Selected Latin American One-Act Plays

❧ Selected
Latin
American
One-Act
Plays

Edited and Translated by
FRANCESCA COLECCHIA
and
JULIO MATAS

University of Pittsburgh Press

862.041
C67s
88475
april 1974

Library of Congress Catalog Card Number 72–92696
ISBN 0–8229–3264–4 (cloth)
ISBN 0–8229–5241–6 (paper)

Contents

Acknowledgments

THE AUTHORS are indebted to Professor Edward Dudley, of the Department of Hispanic Languages and Literatures of the University of Pittsburgh, and Harriet Frey, whose careful reading of the manuscript proved invaluable to them. They also wish to express their appreciation to Constance Tomko, Carolyn Wilson, and Ambrosina Colecchia, who graciously typed the many revisions of the manuscript until it reached its final form.

*   *   *

Grateful acknowledgment is made to the following for permission to translate and publish the plays in this volume:

Fondo de Cultura Económica (Mexico D. F.), for the copyrights of *Parece mentira (Incredible Though It Seems)*, by Xavier Villaurrutia.

Universidad Veracruzana, Departamento Editorial (Xalapa, Mexico), for *Un hogar sólido (A Solid Home)*, by Elena Garro, and *Dialogues* (chosen from *La calle de la gran ocasión*), by Luisa Josefina Hernández.

Escelicer, S. A. (Madrid, Spain), for *Amaos los unos sobre los otros (Love Yourselves Above All Others)*, by Jorge Díaz. Published originally under the title *La pancarta*.

Gustavo Andrade Rivera, Carlos Solórzano, Osvaldo Dragún, Matías Montes Huidobro, Román Chalbaud, and Julio Matas, for their respective plays.

Introduction

THE HISTORY of the theater in Latin America[1] dates from the pre-Columbian period. Chronicles and memoirs of the sixteenth and seventeenth centuries indicate the existence of dramatic activities among the indigenous peoples prior to the arrival of the Spaniard. In the more advanced civilizations—notably the Incan, Aztec, and Mayan—masks, dramatic enclosures with centrally placed stages, a chorus, and rudimentary stage settings were utilized. One can only conjecture upon the degree of refinement this native theater might have attained had its development not been abruptly cut short by the arrival of the conquistadores. The Spanish viewed these dramatic manifestations as the fruits of a pagan culture which had to be discouraged. As a result, performances were for the most part forbidden, and manuscripts destroyed. Even oral tradition became hazardous; thus little if anything was left for the scholar's consideration. One outstanding example of the pre-Columbian drama that has persisted to our day is the Mayan play *Rabinal Achí*.

The conquistadores came accompanied by the priest, whose missionary ardor acknowledged no barriers. The sixteenth-century cleric frequently utilized the dramatic ingenuity of the Indians for his own purposes, and this practice resulted in a religious theater didactical as well as catechetical in nature. In the accounts left by these priests we find commentaries on the dramatizations of Christian beliefs—scenes often in the language of the natives, written for and acted by the Indians. While the essence of this theater was purely Old World,

1. Throughout this work we have favored the expression *Latin America* (and *Latin American*), because it is the most commonly used in present-day English to designate areas of the American continent colonized by peoples with a strong Latin heritage (Spanish, Portuguese, French). We wish to stress here that we have confined ourselves, regarding the material selected, to our field of specialization—Hispanic civilization and literature.

many of the details were from the New World. The end product was
clearly a colorful hybrid of Indian staging of Old and New Testament
stories—Adam and Eve with ocelots, gold and plumed props, and
native costume.

In the second half of the century, with the vigor and intensity of
the missionary theater somewhat diminished, the *teatro criollo*[2]—
the work of native authors other than the Indian—came into view.
Attuned to the character of the new American man, the *teatro criollo*
responded more accurately to his spirit than did either the religious
plays of the missionaries or the emerging European Renaissance
theater. Never to be a pale imitation of the Spanish stage, the *teatro
criollo* strived for its own uniqueness. In so doing, it gave us the
earliest foundations of what would eventually become a genuinely
Latin American theater.

Two names stand out in this theater of the early colonial period—
Cristóbal de Llerena and Fernán González de Eslava. Only one work
of the former, a religious from Santo Domingo, has survived to our
time—an *entremés*.[3] The criticism of colonial officials implicit in
this piece earned its author a period of exile. Fernán González de
Eslava, though born in Seville, spent the major part of his life in
Mexico. Over twenty of his works have come down to us. Re-
nowned in his time for his literary gifts, González de Eslava is acknowledged by most authorities to be the foremost playwright of
Latin America in the sixteenth century.

In the seventeenth century, with the stabilization of the colonial
regime and the subsequent general prosperity, an upper class of
bureaucrats, professionals, landowners, merchants, and ecclesiastics
sprung up in the capitals as well as the centers of trade. This new
aristocracy replaced the crusading zeal of the conquistador and the
missionary with a love of quiet formalities, elegant ceremonies, and

2. In Latin America the term *criollo* referred to a person of all Spanish blood,
born in the New World.
3. A short play, light in tone, usually presented between the acts of a longer
play.

lavish entertainments. The theater occupied a major place among the diversions sponsored by this group. Ships from Europe brought to Latin America not only merchandise, but also books containing the plays of dramatists of the Spanish Golden Age—Lope de Vega, Tirso de Molina, and Calderón de la Barca—and repertory companies to perform these pieces for the colonials. Consequently the sway of the great Spanish dramatists of the period overshadowed the attempts to create a native theater. Those playwrights who did exist in Latin America composed their works according to the formulas of the Spanish drama in vogue at the time. The outstanding figures of this epoch were the Mexicans Juan Ruiz de Alarcón[4] and Sor Juana Inés de la Cruz.

This situation remained relatively unchanged during the greater part of the eighteenth century. The Golden Age repertory, which still enjoyed favor, was augmented by European tragedies and comedies of the neoclassic school.

Of special relevance is the renewed interest in the Indian heritage evinced at the end of the eighteenth century by the performance of three dramas written all or in part in Quechua—*Ollantay*, *The Tragedy of Atahualpa's End*, and *Usca Páucar*. Although patterned upon Spanish models, these plays reflect a native mood associated with the growing unrest which later led to uprisings of the Indian and criollo populations. In the audience, during the 1780 performance of *Ollantay*, which takes its inspiration from Inca tradition, was Tupac Amaru II, the Inca who headed a major rebellion against the Spanish later that year. *The Tragedy of Atahualpa's End* presents this historic event from the Indian point of view, while *Usca Páucar* shows direct influence of continental drama. A fusion of the aboriginal and the Spanish Catholic cultures, this piece tells of the miraculous salvation by the Virgin of an Indian who, like Doctor Faustus, had sold his soul to the devil.

At the beginning of the nineteenth century, the first struggles

4. Though born in Mexico, Ruiz de Alarcón went to Spain where he achieved his success as a dramatist.

for independence erupted. The immediate causes are well known—injustices of the colonial governments, administrative corruption, and the political situation of the Spanish peninsula during and after the Napoleonic war. To these factors were added the diffusion of Enlightenment ideas and the example of the American and French revolutions. Although independence in Latin America resulted in the birth of nations organized along new political lines, it did not bring a complete break from traditional ways, nor from three-hundred-year-old cultural ties with the mother country.

In literature, romanticism became the order of the day. Romantic playwrights, French as well as Spanish, succeeded the neoclassicists as idols of the stage in the 1830s, and their Latin American counterparts existed. With the exception of the plays of the Mexican Fernando Calderón and the Cuban-born Gertrudis Gómez de Avellaneda, most of their works have been either lost or condemned to well-merited oblivion.

More significant, perhaps, in the evolution toward a national drama were plays dealing with everyday life, like the comedies of the Peruvians Felipe Pardo and Manuel Ascensio Segura. Rural farces in Argentina, satirical sketches of contemporary customs in Cuba, the *jíbaro*[5] plays of the Puerto Rican Ramón Méndez Quiñones, and the *sainetes*[6] of the Chilean Román Vidal, appearing almost simultaneously, were typical manifestations of this genre.

In recent years there has been an increasing interest in the narrative literature of Latin America as evidenced by the many translations of novels and short stories available to the non-Spanish-speaking reader. This emphasis on the narrative rather than poetry or drama is the inevitable result of the many fiction writers who have produced remarkable works within the last forty or fifty years in Latin America. Though less widely known, Latin American poetry has also enjoyed a long tradition of quality. While poetry and narrative have received international recognition and boast of several

5. A hillbilly type.
6. A one-act play generally comic in tone, portraying everyday life.

Nobel prizes in literature, Latin American theater remains largely unknown.

The road to a mature, native Latin American theater—comparable today in every way to its contemporaries in other countries—has been long and arduous. As a rule, the production of good dramatic pieces demands the prior existence of a live theater movement, that is, of an appropriate stage where the playwright can confront an audience and, in the process, experiment, learn, and find his own mode of expression in the only way open to him—practice of the art of the theater. Due to varying combinations of commonly known political and economic conditions in Latin America, this development did not happen to any great extent until very recently.

The principal source of theatrical activity until the early twentieth century was the European professional companies, Spanish for the most part, that toured Latin America. They were, however, relatively few in number and removed from the mainstream of Latin American thought and sentiment.

In many Latin American countries, efforts to develop a national theater became a major concern in the first two decades of the 1900s. These attempts met with little success because their fruits suffered from narrow provincialism and lack of perspective. If this theater hoped to achieve significance and status not only within but beyond its continental boundaries, more was required.

After World War I new efforts to revive the Latin American theater, directed to awakening the interest of the public and to creating a drama universal in appeal yet national in inspiration, became evident. They did not originate with the professional stage but with experimental theater groups that had sprung up. These organizations produced not only the works of native authors but also translations of outstanding foreign playwrights—among them Pirandello, Shaw, Lorca, and Giraudoux—thus bringing artistic innovations realized in the theater elsewhere in the world to the Latin American stage. The true value of these groups, however, lay in their stimulus of national dramatic literatures by affording the incipient dramatist the opportunity to stage his works.

The upsurge in dramatic activity of all kinds which characterized the post–World War II theater in Latin America reveals not only a marked increase in the number of plays presented but also an improvement in their quality. Many dramatists became aware of artistic possibilities rarely utilized before, while directors, actors, and designers continued perfecting their craft. The theater was moving rapidly toward assuming its position as a legitimate facet of Latin American letters.

This growth did not progress at the same rate in every country of Latin America. In many places political and economic factors that had inhibited the development of a dramatic tradition in the past still persisted into the twentieth century. Guatemala is a case in point. Hobbled by dependence on a one-crop (coffee) economy, it was further impeded in its cultural growth by the tyrannical dictatorship of Estrada Cabrera (1898–1910) followed, after a brief respite, by that of Jorge Ubico (1931–1944). The more optimistic future for the theater, forecast in the presidencies of Juan José Arévalo (1945–1950) and Jacobo Arbenz (1950–1954), vanished in the upheaval that put the dictator Castillo Armas in power. Because of these and similar circumstances, those signs of change which had appeared earlier on the stage in several Latin American cultural centers did not do so in Guatemala until much later. Two playwrights stand out in modern Guatemalan theater: Carlos Solórzano*[7] and Manuel Galich. In spite of conditions which still seem unfavorable to further theatrical expansion, some recent occurrences give cause for optimism. In 1962 the first Festival de Teatro was held, followed by the founding of the Teatro Juvenil de Vanguardia.

The debilitating effects of adverse politico-economic conditions upon the growth of the theater did not limit themselves to the smaller nations. At the turn of the century, Bogotá, once numbered among the literary centers of Latin America, could not boast of even a brief theater season. Conditions in Colombia prompted Luis Enrique Oso-

---

7. An asterisk (*) indicates that a work by the author is found in this volume.

rio, one of her leading dramatic writers, to declare in 1929 in the preface to his play *El iluminado*: "A Colombian has no excuse for writing a play. He will never see it performed."[8] Osorio, whose works total five volumes ranging from social commentary to political satire and light comedy, not only wrote plays, but also organized a theater company, founded a theater quarterly, and served as both an actor and a director.

In a short-lived effort to stimulate interest in the theater, in 1941 the Colombian government established several open-air theaters throughout the nation. The troubled political situation of the following decade and the consequent economic difficulties in staging their works caused many playwrights to turn to radio and, later, to television, as alternate mediums for their labors. However, in Colombia, as elsewhere, the renaissance of the theater depended primarily upon the experimental theater groups. From the early sixties, the continuing efforts of these groups as well as those of dramatists like Oswaldo Díaz Díaz, Enrique Buenaventura, and Gustavo Andrade Rivera* have lent support to the future of the theater in Colombia.

Mexico, one of the first theater capitals in colonial times, boasting the performance of a play as early as 1526—seven years after Cortez had reached its shores—stands foremost among the centers of dramatic activity in Latin America. In the first decades of the present century two events served as catalysts for the revival of the Mexican theater: the Revolution of 1910 and World War I. Though the First World War allowed for new cultural contacts with Europe, the revolution, which restructured the whole of Mexican society, had a greater bearing on her drama.

As noted earlier, credit for the realization of change must go to the experimental theater groups that were independent of the professional stage. In 1926 El Grupo de los Siete, founded by seven dramatists concerned about the state of the theater in Mexico, initi-

8. Willis Knapp Jones, *Behind Spanish American Footlights* (Austin: University of Texas Press, 1966), p. 332.

ated a concerted effort to broaden the Mexican theater-going public's perspective and raise the quality of stage productions. Groups
such as the Teatro Ulises and the Teatro de Orientación counted
upon the dedication of such playwrights as Xavier Villaurrutia,*
Celestino Gorostiza, Rodolfo Usigli, and Salvador Novo. Usigli is
perhaps the one dramatist who has contributed most to the vitality
of the Mexican theater. As a playwright, producer, translator, and
teacher, he has definitively influenced both the shape and the direction of the modern Mexican stage. The experimental theater still
appears importantly as a medium for the budding writer. Notwith-
standing minor governmental censorship as late as 1969, the Mexican stage remains vigorous and forward-looking. Today the works
of contemporary dramatists of the caliber of Emilio Carballido, Luisa
Josefina Hernández,* Jorge Ibargüengoitia, and Elena Garro* alternate regularly with those of major foreign playwrights during the
theater season.

In Argentina, a remarkable flourishing of national theater with a
rural setting emerged in the 1890s. The gaucho, long the subject of
various sketches and narrative poems, came to the theater in *Juan
Moreira*, an adaptation of Eduardo Gutiérrez's novel of the same
name, first as a circus pantomime in 1884 and later as a play. Similar
plays with a more complex approach to nonurban problems, written
by both Argentine and Uruguayan playwrights, followed on the
heels of *Juan Moreira*. Of particular note among these dramatists is
Florencio Sánchez, whose *M'hijo el doctor*, *La gringa*, and *Barranca
abajo* still rank as masterpieces of that school.

A decline in the artistic level of the dramatic pieces that found their
way to the Argentine stage was followed in the 1930s by a new kind
of dramatic creativity. This activity derived principally from the es-
tablishment of the first independent theaters in Buenos Aires, Teatro
del Pueblo and Teatro La Máscara, which made it possible for leading Argentine dramatic writers like Samuel Eichelbaum and Conrado
Nalé Roxlo to see their works staged. The strengthening of the independent theater movement in the following three decades brought
to the fore a number of talented playwrights such as Carlos Go-

rostiza, Augustín Cuzzani, Osvaldo Dragún,* and more recently, Griselda Gambaro—all of whom deal, from different points of view, with the problems confronting man in an impersonal technocratic world.

Though Chile enjoyed a relatively greater social stability than most countries of Latin America during the early part of the century, significant growth in her theater did not occur until the 1940s. The creation of theater groups at the Universidad de Chile and the Universidad Católica in 1941 and 1943, respectively, was a turning point in the unfolding of Chilean theater. The professional quality attained by these groups and the training they provided led to the organization of similar ensembles throughout the country. Known to many non-Chileans are contemporary authors such as Luis Alberto Heiremans, who attained international recognition with his contemporary version of the legend of the Magi (*Versos de ciego*), Egón Wolff, whose talent is most evident in his dreamlike vision of a revolt of the deprived (*Los invasores*), and Jorge Díaz.*

The general affluence of the post-World War II Venezuelan economy, a result of the expansion of the oil industry, has brought about a cultural renaissance in that country in which the theater plays an important part. Today, Caracas has a theater life that compares favorably to that of Mexico City and Buenos Aires. Prominent contemporary Venezuelan playwrights include Isaac Chocrón, whose works touch upon aspects of the isolation of modern man, Cesar Rengifo, known mainly for his historical dramas, and Román Chalbaud.*

Despite political disturbances in Cuba between 1928 and 1959, a generally firm financial situation allowed for dramatic renewal, which had taken some tentative steps earlier, to continue at a relatively steady pace. Under the leadership of Luis A. Baralt, in 1936 the Teatro La Cueva began staging masterpieces of the Spanish classical theater as well as modern foreign works. The Seminario de Artes Dramáticas of the Universidad de La Habana and the Academia de Artes Dramáticas initiated their activities in 1941, followed by many experimental and little theaters. In his works, Virgilio Piñera, the most outstanding playwright of the period, revealed the somber realities of Cuba that lay beneath her apparently carefree surface. Plays like his *Electra Garrigó* and *Aire frío* rank among the best of Cuban dramatic literature.

The enthusiasm generated by the ambitious cultural plans of the revolution in 1959 resulted in a flurry of theatrical action. Many new playwrights of considerable talent materialized on the Cuban stage. Among these, José Triana, whose agile exercise in parricide, *La noche de los asesinos,* won him international fame, is the most noteworthy. Unfortunately, strict ideological and economic policies implemented between 1961 and 1962 have restricted further theater progress.

The one-act play, to which this volume limits itself, has figured conspicuously in the repertory of theater groups that revolutionized the stage in their times—such as Antoine's Théâtre Libre in Paris or the justly famed Abbey Theatre in Dublin. Many major dramatists have initiated their careers with short plays, while others have cultivated the genre regularly. Playwrights of the stature of Chekhov, Synge, O'Neill, Wilder, and Tennessee Williams—at one time or another—have written one-act plays. For obvious reasons, the one-act play has found universal favor with amateur performing clubs, experimental theaters, and educational dramatic workshops. Its role in Latin America has been paramount. It served as an effective tool in the artistic revivals of the 1930s, allowing for valuable and intensive experimentation on the part of the playwright. To this day, it remains an indispensable part of the program of community and educational theater groups, whose number in Latin America, in view of the socioeconomic shortcomings, is most impressive.

To our knowledge, this is the first anthology in English of Latin American one-act plays. It is not in the least exhaustive, either in the introductory comments or in the pieces selected. We have limited ourselves to the works of ten authors from seven countries, giving preference to those works which demand simple, yet imaginative stage productions. This and a concern for the overall quality of the collection explain the small number of works chosen. Certain pertinent authors who have cultivated this form, it is true, do not appear here. This omission does not necessarily reflect a negative critical attitude toward their work. It is rather the result either of self-imposed restrictions in our concept of the total collection or of our inability to secure the author's permission to use his work.

The aim of this collection is not only to acquaint the reader with a new and stimulating drama, but also to provide university and community theaters with material which is sufficiently fresh and challenging to merit their performance of it. The plays are arranged according to their dates of publication or composition, beginning with the earliest work. Topics range from the existential dilemma of modern man to social comment and political satire. This same diversity is reflected in the techniques used.

It is our sincere hope that both the reading and the theater-going public will come to know more of this worthy and, heretofore, overlooked aspect of Latin American letters.

F. C. and J. M.

Incredible Though It Seems

Xavier Villaurrutia

(Mexico)

Xavier Villaurrutia

Born in Mexico City in 1903, Xavier Villaurrutia first came to the attention of Mexican literary circles with the inclusion of several of his poems in *Ocho Poetas*, an anthology published in 1923. Eleven years later his first play, *Parece mentira*, was staged. His interest in the theater grew progressively more intense, more all-consuming, but never to the exclusion of his finely crafted verse which he continued to write up to his death on Christmas in 1950. ■ Villaurrutia spent the academic year 1935–36 at Yale University, where he studied dramatic composition and stage technique on a Rockefeller grant. The experience not only heightened his dramatic sensitivity but also confirmed his own creative inclination toward a highly universal rather than a nationally oriented drama like that of other members of his generation (Rodolfo Usigli, Celestino Gorostiza). His efforts in behalf of the Mexican theater did not limit themselves to playwriting. They span the total range of theatrical activity— actor, director, critic, translator, teacher. One of the founders of the Teatro Ulises, the first experimental theater group in Mexico, he also took an active part in the activities of its successor, the prestigious Teatro de Orientación. ■ The theater of Xavier Villaurrutia comprises one-act pieces such as *Parece mentira* (1934), *El ausente* (1943), *Sea usted breve*, *¿En qué piensas?*, *Ha llegado el momento* (all in 1938), as well as traditional three-act plays. The latter include *Invitación a la muerte* (1940), *La hiedra* (1941), *La mujer legítima* (1942), *El solterón* (1945), *El yerro candente* (1945), *El pobre Barba Azul* (1948) *Juego peligroso* (1950), and *La tragedia de las equivocaciones* (1950). ■ *Incredible Though It Seems* (*Parece mentira*), found in this volume, is most aptly described by its subtitle, *Enigma en un acto*. The struggle of its characters with the questions of identity and purpose in this unsolved mystery reflects the generally existentialist orientation of the Mexican dramatist's theater. Villaurrutia's drama reveals the strong influences of leading modern European playwrights such as Pirandello, Cocteau, Giraudoux, and Anouilh. Though the author's poetry makes his preoccupation with death seem paramount, his theater gives us the opposite side of the coin as he plumbs the essence of being.

Incredible Though It Seems
A Riddle in One Act

Characters

THE EMPLOYEE
A HUSBAND
A BUSYBODY
AN ATTORNEY
FIRST WOMAN
SECOND WOMAN
THIRD WOMAN

Time: Present
Place: Waiting room in the office of an ATTORNEY

(The room appears empty. Pause. The bell of the door at the rear, left, is heard. The EMPLOYEE *appears through the door at the right. He opens the door, and the* HUSBAND—*uncertain, timid, enters.)*

HUSBAND: Mr. Fernández? Attorney Fernández?

EMPLOYEE *(automatically, thinking of something else)*: He hasn't arrived yet. Come in and wait for him.

HUSBAND: I had an appointment for . . .

EMPLOYEE *(interrupting him)*: Come in and wait for him.

HUSBAND: . . . seven o'clock.

EMPLOYEE: Have a seat.

HUSBAND: . . . only that, rather than having an appointment with Mr. Fernández, I was notified to be here and I don't know . . .

EMPLOYEE: The attorney won't be long in arriving.

3

HUSBAND: . . . and I don't know if I should remain here without explaining to Mr. Fernández the reason for my presence in his office.

EMPLOYEE (*cuttingly*): The attorney will be very pleased to hear you.

(*The* EMPLOYEE *bows and leaves by the door at the left. The* HUSBAND *looks for the least visible chair and occupies it. Pause. The doorbell is heard. The* EMPLOYEE *reappears. He opens the door and the* BUSYBODY *appears.*)

BUSYBODY: I'd like to speak with Attorney Fernández.

EMPLOYEE: Come in and wait for him. (*He puts the* BUSYBODY's *hat on the clothes tree.*)

HUSBAND (*getting up and wanting to explain the reason for his presence to the* EMPLOYEE): Do you think that Mr. Fernández will not have any objections . . .?

EMPLOYEE (*interrupting him*): None. (*To the* BUSYBODY:) You can sit down if you like.

BUSYBODY (*who has not seen the* HUSBAND): Am I the first person who has come to see him this afternoon?

EMPLOYEE: The first one after the gentleman. (*He says this indicating the* HUSBAND. *The* BUSYBODY *and the latter exchange that first fierce glance of persons condemned to occupy the same cage for some time. The* BUSYBODY *sits down. The telephone rings. The* EMPLOYEE *picks up the receiver.*) Yes. . . . No, he hasn't arrived yet. . . . Yes, every afternoon. . . . At seven. . . . We're accustomed to considering seven afternoon . . . I can't tell you exactly. Yes, sir. . . . His home address? We aren't authorized to reveal it. At your service. (*He hangs up the receiver. He gets ready to leave.*)

BUSYBODY (*standing*): Excuse me, just a word.

EMPLOYEE: Yes.

BUSYBODY: Mr. Fernández, is he young?

EMPLOYEE: Within a few minutes you'll be able to tell me if he looks so to you.

BUSYBODY: I'd like to know your opinion.

EMPLOYEE: My points of view are, surely, different from yours. Like as not, the person who seems young to me will seem like Methuselah to you.

BUSYBODY: Then, and don't misjudge me, how young is he by comparison?

EMPLOYEE: Compared with Mr. Fernández's father, Mr. Fernández is young. Compared with Mr. Fernández's son, Mr. Fernández is no longer young.

BUSYBODY: You're a master in the art of not committing yourself.

EMPLOYEE: Pardon me, but I don't understand you.

BUSYBODY: There's no doubt about it, you're the perfect private secretary.

EMPLOYEE: I'm not the attorney's private secretary.

BUSYBODY: And, nevertheless, you act as if you were.

EMPLOYEE: Mr. Fernández has no secrets. Why should he have a secretary? I take care of the telephones. I receive the clients. I've no other duties. I'm a simple employee.

BUSYBODY: I think that you would deserve . . .

EMPLOYEE (*interrupting him gently*): No one has what he deserves. Right now, perhaps you deserve my satisfying your curiosity. (*The* BUSYBODY's *eyes shine.*) But if I were to do so, it would be unjust, in the first place, to the attorney who doesn't deserve to have an indiscreet reply put him in a compromising situation and, in the second place, to myself.

BUSYBODY: To yourself?

EMPLOYEE: Yes, because, and forgive me if I emphasize in passing your injustice, haven't you thought that with your questions you rob me of time that I don't deserve to lose?

BUSYBODY: Do you have a lot of work?

(*The* EMPLOYEE *smiles. He seems to be interested in the conversation. He takes a seat.*)

EMPLOYEE: I'm not referring to the time that we employ in a manual task like putting together a file or using the Xerox machine, time that in the end we can recover again after some kind of delay and without considerable loss. Think of the time that we take from the development of an idea, from the continuity of a monologue, from the return of a precious memory, which, once interrupted, escapes and hides in the attic of our minds to reappear who knows when.

BUSYBODY: Are you a poet?

EMPLOYEE: Your impressions go from one extreme to another, without passing through the center. A moment ago I seemed a private secretary to you, now a poet.

BUSYBODY: The fault isn't mine. You keep silent like a private secretary and you speak like a poet.

EMPLOYEE: It's true. And I'm happy to find a person to whom a single glance and some few words have given the key to my ambivalence.

BUSYBODY: Ambivalence?

EMPLOYEE: Don't be frightened. . . . It's the modern name for an ancient phenomenon which you yourself have just experienced by making a double judgment on my manner of being.

BUSYBODY: Then you believe . . . ?

EMPLOYEE: I believe that in each one of us exist, simultaneously, contradictory feelings toward the same thing, toward the same person . . .

BUSYBODY: Ah, yes. That business of love and hate . . .

EMPLOYEE: If you wish. And, more still, double ways of being that, as in my case, are apparently inimical.

BUSYBODY: Only apparently?

EMPLOYEE: In my case the employee and the poet shake hands. However, the most frequent thing is the ignorance of these duplicities of the personality.

BUSYBODY: But isn't it easy to know them?

EMPLOYEE: On the contrary, man lives and dies not knowing himself. All of his life, or almost all of it, he spends doing everything possible not to recognize that in reality he isn't one man, but two or more. He plays hide-and-seek with himself. Even knowing where he hides he doesn't dare to say, "Here I am," or, "Here is the other one." You, just like that, without thinking, have attributed to me two such different beings, that of the employee and that of the poet —have you admitted to yourself how many and which are your simultaneous lives?

BUSYBODY: The truth is that I've never even thought of it.

EMPLOYEE: I advise you to dare to do so. Perhaps in the awareness of that plurality you may find what we call happiness, or comfort, or, at least, the explanation of your torments.

BUSYBODY: And if I were to tell you that I'm happy and that I don't need to explain to myself the torments that I don't suffer?

EMPLOYEE: If that were true, on declaring it you would only demonstrate your nonexistence. But you yourself haven't dared to assert categorically that you're happy and that you're resigned to your kind of life.

(*During the dialogue between the* EMPLOYEE *and the* BUSYBODY, *the* HUSBAND *begins to show signs of uneasiness. Neither the* EMPLOYEE *nor the* BUSYBODY *is aware of the presence of the third person.*)

HUSBAND (*drawing strength from his timidity*): Gentlemen . . . (*The* EMPLOYEE *and the* BUSYBODY *notice that they have been speaking in front of a third party. Once their first astonishment at this has passed, they exchange a glance which is a complete pact. The* HUSBAND *draws his chair near, without getting up entirely, and continues.*) Gentlemen, . . . I don't know if I should. I don't know if with this interruption I stupidly cut off a dialogue that, in any other case, I'd have respected by pretending, as is my duty, not to hear. However, it happens that (*Addressing the* BUSYBODY) you spoke a moment ago of a happy being, self-satisfied and ignorant of any torment, . . . and you (*Addressing the* EMPLOYEE) suggested the possibility that that type of man may not exist.

BUSYBODY: So it is.

EMPLOYEE: So it is. (*Standing.*)

HUSBAND: Well, then, if I'd had the pleasure of knowing you twenty-four hours ago, I'd have been able to tell you that I was that man. (*Now it is the* BUSYBODY *who draws near to the* HUSBAND). The well-being, the comfort, the good economic circumstances and a well-balanced happiness were within me and outside of me. And let's say not a torment, not even the slightest worry darkened my thoughts or my habits. . . .

BUSYBODY (*triumphantly*): In a word, you weren't existing. (*He sits down.*)

HUSBAND: Rather, I was unaware that I existed.

BUSYBODY: And now?

HUSBAND: Now . . . (*Backing out morally and materially*) now I can't say anything else. (*He sits down.*)

EMPLOYEE (*after an exchange of glances with the* BUSYBODY, *insinuatingly*): For what reasons? Nothing prevented us from speaking with all frankness, an instant ago, in front of you.

BUSYBODY: It's true.

EMPLOYEE: Your silence just now reveals a distrust, a reserve . . .

HUSBAND: You forget that we scarcely know each other . . . that strictly speaking, we don't know each other.

EMPLOYEE: Not only do I not forget it, but, in fact, it's the only thing that I take into account. Thanks to the fact that we don't know each other, this exchange of intimacies has been possible between persons who, precisely because nothing binds them, have nothing to hide. The interest which you have demonstrated by intervening suddenly in our conversation has betrayed you.

HUSBAND (*cowardly*): It was an accident.

EMPLOYEE: The fact is that you accidentally interrupted in order to begin to unburden yourself, to free yourself of something you can't hold in any more.

HUSBAND: Anyway, I've more than one friend in whom to confide. . . .

EMPLOYEE: Allow me to believe only the first part of your sentence. You probably have one or many friends, but you're not going to confide in them what you yourself wouldn't even want to think.

HUSBAND: What are friends for, then?

EMPLOYEE: A friend is someone to whom we relate our victories and from whom we hide our defeats. I know situations like yours, and although fortune hasn't given me the opportunity to experience them personally, I've lived these situations intensely . . . in others. (*The doorbell is heard. The clients return to their places and adopt attitudes of indifference. The* EMPLOYEE *recovers the personality of an employee. He opens the door.*) Come in, madam. (*The* FIRST WOMAN, *a young woman, dressed in black, her face covered by a veil, enters. The* FIRST WOMAN *takes from her purse a card which she gives to the* EMPLOYEE. *The* EMPLOYEE, *with mechanical courtesy, bows and leads the* FIRST WOMAN *to the door of the private office at the right, inviting her to enter.*) This way, please. (*The* FIRST WOMAN *enters the private office. The* EMPLOYEE *returns to the chairs and takes a seat. The* BUSY-BODY *has drawn his chair closer again. Everything is as it was before the arrival of the* FIRST WOMAN.) And although fortune hasn't given me the opportunity to experience them personally, I've lived these situations intensely . . . in others. (*The doorbell is heard. All of the movement of persons and things is repeated. After opening the door, the* EMPLOYEE *speaks.*) Come in, madam. (*A* SECOND WOMAN *enters, identical to the previous one. She takes a card from her purse and gives it to the* EMPLOYEE *who invites her to enter the private office.*) This way, please. (*The* SECOND WOMAN *enters the private office. When the* EMPLOYEE *approaches his seat, the* HUSBAND, *who has turned progressively and mortally paler before the repeated appearances of the women, wants to say something which finally chokes itself in his throat. The* EMPLOYEE *and the* BUSYBODY *do not notice any of this. The former has again taken his chair. The* BUSYBODY *has drawn his chair close and awaits, like an oracle, the words of the* EMPLOYEE.) And although fortune hasn't given me the opportunity to experience them personally, I've lived these situations intensely . . . in others. (*For the third time, the ringing of the doorbell is heard. The* BUSYBODY *and the* EMPLOYEE *unconsciously repeat the same gestures and movements. Everything again occupies its original place, except that the* HUSBAND *remains like a statue when he hears the voice of the* EM-PLOYEE *and the* THIRD WOMAN *appears and enters, identical to the two previous ones. One would almost swear that she is also the same one. She gives a card to the* EMPLOYEE *and the latter repeats the previous gestures and actions.*) This way, if you please.

THIRD WOMAN: Don't bother, I know the way.

(*The* THIRD WOMAN *enters the private office. The* EMPLOYEE *closes the door, and just as he returns to his seat he looks at the* HUSBAND, *who struggles to speak and only emits a sort of groan.*)

EMPLOYEE: What's happening to you? What's happening to you?

BUSYBODY: He's choking! He's choking!

EMPLOYEE: Calm yourself, calm yourself.

BUSYBODY: A little water is good in these cases.

HUSBAND (*finally managing to speak*): Who is she? . . . (*To the* EMPLOYEE:) Who is that woman?

BUSYBODY: Which of the three?

HUSBAND (*seizing the lapel of the* EMPLOYEE's *jacket, in an agitated voice*): Who is she?

EMPLOYEE (*taking away the* HUSBAND's *hand, he answers him as an employee*): I'm not authorized to reveal it.

HUSBAND (*imploringly*): Answer me, I beg you.

BUSYBODY: Yes, answer him.

HUSBAND: A moment ago you seemed capable of understanding everything. . . . I beg you. Who is that woman?

EMPLOYEE: You're right. Now I ought not to lie, nor to hide, nor hush up anything. Now I should speak the bare truth, instead of talking to you as a hypocritical employee.

HUSBAND (*moved*): Thank you. . . . Who is she?

EMPLOYEE (*disconsolate*): I don't know who she is. I swear it.

BUSYBODY: Which one of the three? Do you want to know their names? Each one of them handed you a card.

HUSBAND: He's right. She handed you a card.

EMPLOYEE: Wait. (*He looks in his pockets. He finds only one card.*)

BUSYBODY: Look for the other two.

EMPLOYEE (*after reading the card*): We're making no progress. She gave me the attorney's card.

BUSYBODY (*taking the card from him*): Two cards are missing.

EMPLOYEE (*looking once more in his pockets*): There are no more.

BUSYBODY (*surprised*): And nevertheless . . .

HUSBAND (*impatiently*): It's useless. . . . I beg you. . . . The woman who has just entered, has she been here on other occasions?

EMPLOYEE: I'll try to remember by all the means that are at my command. I'll tell you the truth, the whole truth. Come with me. (*He goes to the private office, followed closely by the* BUSYBODY *who does not miss the opportunity to prove that he is most interested in the* HUSBAND's *affairs.*) Are you referring to the woman dressed in black, the one with the veil?

BUSYBODY: But, to which one of them?

HUSBAND: Yes, to the woman.

EMPLOYEE: One moment. . . . Yes, it's the same one. I think that it's the same one. The woman has come in search of the lawyer . . . wait . . . two other times. This makes the third time that I've seen her. I'm what is called a bad physiognomist . . . but the woman has always come here the same way, with a veil, that is to say, faceless. I remember that her presence and her silence intrigued me . . . although I'm not sure that it isn't just now that they intrigue me.

HUSBAND: Nevertheless, the woman spoke to you.

EMPLOYEE: Wait. . . . She spoke to me now, but the first and the second time that she came . . . I'd like to remember exactly. What day is today?

BUSYBODY: Monday.

HUSBAND (*eagerly*): Make an effort. Try to remember.

EMPLOYEE: That's it. She came on Monday and then the Monday of the following week. Wait. . . . What time is it?

BUSYBODY: Seven.

EMPLOYEE: Or, rather, she came three days in a row at the same time, at that time . . . or three times the same day.

HUSBAND (*impatiently*): What has she told you? What did she tell you just a moment ago?

EMPLOYEE: She said only, "Don't bother. I know the way."

(*On hearing this sentence, the* HUSBAND *falls dejected into a chair. The two surround him.*)

HUSBAND: "I know the way." There's no doubt. She has come three times. It's she.

EMPLOYEE: Who?

BUSYBODY: Who?

(*The* HUSBAND *doesn't answer. Pause.*)

EMPLOYEE: You can tell everything with the certainty that your grief will be understood and respected. If, as I believe, it's necessary to keep your secret, we'll know how to keep it.

BUSYBODY: Naturally.

EMPLOYEE (*after another pause*): If you don't dare to speak and you're thinking that you need to . . . , I could interpret your feelings with the same words with which you would speak. I'm used to doing that. From the time I was a child, I used to declare the sins committed by others. I have the gift, the secret or ability, sometimes very painful, of making things and beings speak. From their words, I make my poems. From their confessions, my novels. . . . (*The* HUS-

BAND *makes a gesture of astonishment.*) But don't fear, I won't write your novel. It's already written. But that hinders me from leaving you like a shipwrecked person, in the midst of the storm, without bringing you to the shore of a confession that you need. Don't tell me anything. I imagine your case and I regret what I imagine.

HUSBAND: Imagine what I feel!

BUSYBODY (*unable to resist any more*):   Who is she? Who is she?

HUSBAND (*to the* EMPLOYEE): You've guessed it. I read it in your eyes. Tell him. I can't.

EMPLOYEE (*to the* BUSYBODY): You too can read it in my eyes.

(*They exchange a glance. The* BUSYBODY *studies the eyes of the* EMPLOYEE.)

BUSYBODY: Yes, yes. (*Speaking to himself.*) But, which one of the three?

HUSBAND: Now we all know. It was yesterday, at night, thanks to an anonymous letter, to this anonymous letter.

(*He takes out a sheet of paper. The* BUSYBODY *takes hold of it. He devours rather than reads it, and he offers it to the* EMPLOYEE, *who takes it and, without even looking at it, puts it in the hands of the* HUSBAND.)

EMPLOYEE (*sits down. And then, in his most insinuating voice*): It's useless. I know it's impersonal and direct style. From time immemorial man has practiced this literary genre that attains, at times, a classic perfection. At the same time that it says all it has to say, the author remains cowardly invisible. "Appear Monday afternoon in the office of Attorney Fernández and you will be convinced that your wife deceives you before your very eyes."

BUSYBODY (*astonished*): That's it, more or less!

EMPLOYEE: More or less?

BUSYBODY: Less.

EMPLOYEE: Wait. "This will be the third time that your wife has visited Attorney Fernández. She knows the way."

(*The* BUSYBODY *and the* HUSBAND *are bewildered. The anonymous letter says the same thing, neither more nor less.*)

HUSBAND (*standing*): How could you . . . ?

BUSYBODY (*standing*): You've guessed it!

HUSBAND (*suspecting the* EMPLOYEE): One moment. One moment. You didn't guess it.

BUSYBODY: You're right, you're right. It wasn't possible.

HUSBAND (*angrily, shaking the anonymous letter*): You wrote it.

EMPLOYEE: Calm yourself. You're wrong.

HUSBAND (*still angry*): You wrote it. . . . (*However returning to the reality of his situation:*) You knew it all!

EMPLOYEE (*master, more than ever, of himself*): I knew nothing before you arrived, before things happened as they have happened. I'm not the author of the anonymous letter. Nor is there reason to be surprised that I could read it. It's a matter of an anonymous letter like any other. I've written them. Rather, my characters have written them. And the reality of this situation has made it possible for me to literally reproduce the text.

BUSYBODY: It's marvelous!

EMPLOYEE: My friend, the marvelous doesn't exist. The marvelous thing is that the marvelous doesn't exist. That which we judge marvelous is only an acute, evident, bewildering form of the real.

BUSYBODY: But all of this seems incredible!

EMPLOYEE: You've said it. It seems incredible! (*Approaching the* HUSBAND *and putting a hand on his shoulder:*) And as for what concerns you, dear friend, allow me to call you that, think of the comfort and the ignorance in which your life was unfolding as only an empty reality, an uninhabited world, a road without a landscape, a sleep without dreams, in a word, an eternal death. Now, as you yourself have just said, thanks to an anonymous letter, that is, thanks to a revelation, a revelation of a secret, you find yourself on the threshold of an existence that you'll be able to discuss, correct, and manage as you please, in the same way as an artist plans, corrects, and elaborates his work in progress. (*Very short pause.*) And now I have nothing more to tell you. It's up to you to take up the work or to throw it off. I owe nothing. I want nothing. I can advise you on nothing. The only thing left to me is to disappear.

BUSYBODY: You're right. (*He calls the* EMPLOYEE *aside.*) I too ought to withdraw, but, on what pretext? I'd like to find something that gives the impression that I'm not doing him a favor. I wouldn't want to hurt him. . . .

EMPLOYEE: Think of something. . . .

(*Suddenly inspired, the* BUSYBODY *goes toward the* HUSBAND, *and in a happy, unconcerned tone takes leave of him saying:*)

BUSYBODY: Well, gentlemen. My pleasure. Good evening.

HUSBAND (*confused*): Are you going?

BUSYBODY: You won't believe it, but I've forgotten the purpose of my presence in this office. On the other hand, I do remember that at this time I've an important appointment. I'm sure that if I remain longer at your side, I'll also forget that commitment, as I forget everything. I suffer from that illness that the doctors call . . . what do they call it?

EMPLOYEE: Amnesia.

BUSYBODY: That's it, amnesia. Did I say amnesia? . . . Good evening.

(*He bows and he leaves. The* EMPLOYEE *closes the door carefully. The* HUSBAND *finds himself, meanwhile, in the center of the room, standing, uncertain, as at the crossing of two roads, without knowing which road to take. The* EMPLOYEE *approaches slowly. They stand face to face, wordless, motionless. A long pause, as though time had stopped, leaving their figures caught and outlined in a sort of still life. One has the impression that this scene will continue indefinitely unless something indifferent from without comes to interrupt this motionlessness and set the gears in motion again. Finally the bell from the private office is rung.*)

HUSBAND (*shaking himself, he comes to life*): Did you hear?

EMPLOYEE (*awakening*): Yes. (*Without moving, rigid, he answers as an employee.*) I'm coming, right away. (*Then, becoming human, he approaches the* HUSBAND.) Will you believe me if I tell you that I envy you with all my heart, that I would give anything to find myself in your place? . . . You're the producer of a show in which you'll be at the same time playwright, actor, and spectator. Think that I, on the other hand, live miserably like a thief from the fragments of life that I rob from others in moments of distraction, of absentmindedness, or, as now, through the intervention of chance. The same bell that reminds me of my daily death calls you to a new life. (*The bell rings again. Automatically the* EMPLOYEE *answers as an employee.*) I'm coming, right away.

HUSBAND: Wait a moment. I'd like to ask a favor of you.

EMPLOYEE (*becoming human*): Yes.

HUSBAND: I am sure that if you don't go quickly, she'll come out. She's impatient. I can tell by her ringing. I prefer to speak to her here, and, if you permit it, to speak to her without much light.

(*The* EMPLOYEE *turns out the brightest light. The opaque light of an aquarium remains.*)

EMPLOYEE: Is it enough?

HUSBAND: Yes.

EMPLOYEE: Do you want something else?

HUSBAND: Thank you, that's all. (*The telephone rings. The* EMPLOYEE *debates a moment whether to answer or not.*) Answer.

(*The* EMPLOYEE *goes to the telephone. He picks up the receiver and sets it gently on the table.*)

EMPLOYEE: What does the outside world matter to us! Now no one will bother you.

HUSBAND (*moved*): Thanks.

EMPLOYEE: So long, then.

HUSBAND: So long. (*And at the same time that the* EMPLOYEE *leaves through the door at the right, almost to himself:*) Thanks. (*A pause. The door of the private office opens and the* FIRST WOMAN *appears. The* HUSBAND *takes a step toward her. The* FIRST WOMAN *makes a gesture of surprise on finding herself in a place almost without light. She hesitates over whether to return to the private office or to call out. Finally she gets ready to leave, when the* HUSBAND *approaches her and in a voice that wants to be firm says to her:*) Mariana! (*Pause.*) Why have you come? I know it all, thanks to this letter. I could kill you, but your dead body wouldn't feel the vengeance that I have for you. . . . (*The* FIRST WOMAN *surprised, makes a gesture that announces that she is going to speak.*) Not a word. Out of here! At once! Don't speak! Not here! (*Covering her face.*) Not here! (*The* FIRST WOMAN *stifles a cry and leaves, taking advantage of the moment. Pause. When the* HUSBAND *uncovers his face, the door of the private office opens and the* SECOND WOMAN *appears. The* HUSBAND *on seeing her, says in a less sure voice:*) Why have you returned? I don't know whether you've put on that veil to hide your shame or your shamelessness. . . . Look, I too have hidden my face. I've turned out the light. . . . I too am a coward. . . . If only you hadn't returned! Let's leave here. Let's go. . . . If you hadn't returned. (*The*

SECOND WOMAN *stifles a cry as the* FIRST WOMAN *did and leaves rapidly.*) Wait. Wait. (*He looks for his hat. At first he does not find it. At last he finds it. He is going to follow her, but something at his back stops him. It is the* THIRD WOMAN, *who has opened the door of the private office and appears on the threshold. The* HUSBAND, *on seeing her, goes toward her and is overwhelmed, intimidated, and shaking until the end.*) Now you see. Here I am. I can't stop from coming. I spy on you. I wait for you. I follow your footsteps. I haven't been able to take revenge. . . . I kept a constant, daily, secret hate for you . . . , but it has been only a new form of love, more acute and lucid than the other.

(*The* THIRD WOMAN *crosses the room rapidly and before leaving, stifles the same cry. The* HUSBAND *remains, frustrated, motionless, without the strength to follow her, in the middle of the room. Pause. The door at the rear opens and the* ATTORNEY *enters. He is surprised to find the room dark. He goes to the switch and turns on the light. He finds the receiver disconnected. He picks it up and speaks.*)

ATTORNEY: Hello. Hello. (*He hangs up the receiver. He looks surprised at the* HUSBAND *who recovers himself rapidly. It appears that he is going to ask the* HUSBAND *something. He does not do it. He goes to the private office and from the doorway, with a gesture, he invites the* HUSBAND *to enter.*) Come in, please.

HUSBAND: At once, at once. (*And instead of going into the private office, the* HUSBAND *leaves abruptly through the rear door to the surprise of the* ATTORNEY.)

CURTAIN

The Man Who Turned Into a Dog

Osvaldo Dragún

(Argentina)

Osvaldo Dragún

Born in Entre Ríos, Argentina, in 1929, Osvaldo Dragún moved to Buenos Aires in 1945 where he soon became involved with several experimental theater groups. He finally abandoned his university studies to devote himself fully to the theater. In 1956 Fray Mocho, an independent theater group famed throughout Latin America for the high caliber of its productions, presented his first work, *La peste viene de Melos*—an uneven piece using the Athenian invasion of Melos during the Peloponnesian Wars as the background for a study of dubious imperialistic designs. A year later this same company presented his *Túpac Amaru*, an excellent historical play about the famous Inca chief of the same name who led an ill-fated rebellion against the Spanish colonial rule in the eighteenth century. Dragún transcends simple historical fact in this piece, converting his hero into a symbol of the spiritual superiority of the individual over an oppressive social system. ■ *Historias para ser contadas* (1956), a series of one-act plays, the last of which has been selected for this anthology, offers a set of imaginative sketches depicting—in a clownesque style which, by contrast, enhances their essentially tragic spirit—the consequences of having to conform to the norms of today's dehumanized world. Death, debasement, guilt, serve as themes of these brilliant short plays. Much of Dragún's fame outside of Argentina can be attributed to this group of short pieces. They have been performed in major cities around the globe, including the Theater Festival of Nations in Paris. *Milagro en el mercado viejo* took first prize in 1963 in the annual competition sponsored by the Casa de las Américas in Havana. Dragún's *Heroica de Buenos Aires* received the first prize three years later in the same contest. ■ The Argentinian playwright's dramatic works include *Los de la mesa diez* (1957), *Historia de mi esquina* (1958), *El jardín del infierno* (1960), *Y nos dijeron que éramos inmortales* (1961), *Amoretta* (1964), and *Un maldito sábado* (1968), all of which denounce certain evils prevalent in Latin American society—corruption of traditional institutions, insensitivity of the entrenched older generations, and purposeless violence. In his dramatic technique, especially in his latest plays, the influence of Bertolt Brecht is most evident.

The Man Who Turned Into a Dog

Characters
FIRST ACTOR
SECOND ACTOR
THIRD ACTOR
ACTRESS

SECOND ACTOR: Friends, let's tell the story this way . . .

THIRD ACTOR: The way they told it to us this afternoon.

ACTRESS: It's the tale of "The Man Who Turned Into a Dog."

THIRD ACTOR: It began two years ago on a bench in a square. There, sir . . . , where today you were trying to fathom the secret of a leaf.

ACTRESS: There, where stretching out our arms, we held the world by its head and its feet, and said to it, "Play, accordion, play!"

SECOND ACTOR: We met him there. (FIRST ACTOR *enters.*) He was . . . (*He points to the* FIRST ACTOR.) . . . the way you see him, nothing more. And he was very sad.

ACTRESS: He became our friend. He was looking for work, and we were actors.

THIRD ACTOR: He had to support his wife, and we were actors.

SECOND ACTOR: He would dream of life, and he would awaken during the night, screaming. And we were actors.

ACTRESS: He became our friend, of course. Just like that. . . . (*She points to him.*) Nothing more.

ALL: And he was very sad!

THIRD ACTOR: Time went by. Fall . . .

SECOND ACTOR: Summer . . .

ACTRESS: Winter . . .

THIRD ACTOR: Spring . . .

FIRST ACTOR: Lie! I never knew spring.

SECOND ACTOR: Fall . . .

ACTRESS: Winter . . .

THIRD ACTOR: Summer. And we returned. And we went to visit him because he was our friend.

SECOND ACTOR: And we asked, "Is he all right?" And his wife told us . . .

ACTRESS: I don't know . . .

THIRD ACTOR: Is he sick?

ACTRESS: I don't know.

SECOND AND THIRD ACTORS: Where is he?

ACTRESS: In the dog pound.

(FIRST ACTOR *enters on all fours*.)

SECOND AND THIRD ACTORS: Uhh!

THIRD ACTOR (*observing him*):
          I am the director of the pound.
          And that's okay with me.
          He arrived barking like a dog
          (the main requirement).
          Even if he wears a suit,
          he is a dog, beyond a doubt.

SECOND ACTOR (*stuttering*):
    I am the veterinarian,
    and th-this is cl-clear to me.
    Al-although he s-seems a man,
    wh-what is here is a d-dog.

FIRST ACTOR (*to the audience*): And I, what can I tell you? I don't
know whether I'm a man or a dog. And I believe that in the end not
even you will be able to tell me. Because it all began in the most
ordinary fashion. I went to a factory to look for a job. I hadn't found
anything in three months, and I went there to look for work.

THIRD ACTOR: Didn't you read the sign? There Are No Openings.

FIRST ACTOR: Yes, I read it. Don't you have anything for me?

THIRD ACTOR: If it says There Are No Openings, there are none.

FIRST ACTOR: Of course. Don't you have anything for me?

THIRD ACTOR: Not for you, not for the president!

FIRST ACTOR: Okay. Don't you have anything for me?

THIRD ACTOR: No!

FIRST ACTOR: Lathe operator . . .

THIRD ACTOR: No!

FIRST ACTOR: Mechanic . . .

THIRD ACTOR: No!

FIRST ACTOR: S[ecretary] . . .

THIRD ACTOR: No!

FIRST ACTOR: Er[rand boy] . . .

THIRD ACTOR: N[o]!

FIRST ACTOR: F[oreman] . . .

THIRD ACTOR: N[o]!

FIRST ACTOR: Night watchman! Night watchman! Even if it's just a night watchman!

ACTRESS (*as if she were playing a horn*): Toot, toot, toooot. The boss! (*The* SECOND *and* THIRD ACTORS *make signs to each other.*)

THIRD ACTOR (*to the audience*): Ladies and gentlemen, the night watchman's dog had died the night before, after twenty-five years of dedication.

SECOND ACTOR: He was a very old dog.

ACTRESS: Amen.

SECOND ACTOR (*to the* FIRST ACTOR): Do you know how to bark?

FIRST ACTOR: Lathe operator.

SECOND ACTOR: Do you know how to bark?

FIRST ACTOR: Mechanic . . .

SECOND ACTOR: Do you know how to bark?

FIRST ACTOR: Bricklayer . . .

SECOND AND THIRD ACTORS: There are no openings!

FIRST ACTOR (*pausing*): Bowwow . . . Bowwow! . . .

SECOND ACTOR: Very good, I congratulate you . . .

THIRD ACTOR: We'll give you ten pesos a day, the doghouse, and your food.

SECOND ACTOR: As you see, he earned ten pesos a day more than the real dog.

ACTRESS: When he returned home, he told me of the job he had gotten. He was drunk.

FIRST ACTOR (*to his wife*): But they promised me that as soon as the first worker would retire, die, or be fired, they would give me his job. Amuse yourself, Maria, amuse yourself! Bowwow . . . bowwow! . . . Amuse yourself, Maria, amuse yourself.

SECOND AND THIRD ACTORS: Bowwow . . . bowwow . . . Amuse yourself, Maria, amuse yourself!

ACTRESS: He was drunk, poor dear . . .

FIRST ACTOR: And the following night I began to work. . . . (*He gets down on all fours.*)

SECOND ACTOR: Is the doghouse too small for you?

FIRST ACTOR: I can't stoop so much.

THIRD ACTOR: Does it crowd you here?

FIRST ACTOR: Yes.

THIRD ACTOR: All right, but look, don't tell me yes. You must begin to get used to the new you. Tell me, bowwow . . . bowwow! . . .

SECOND ACTOR: Does it crowd you here? (*The* FIRST ACTOR *does not answer.*) Does it crowd you here?

FIRST ACTOR: Bowwow . . . bowwow! . . .

SECOND ACTOR: Fine . . . (*He leaves.*)

FIRST ACTOR: But that night it rained, and I had to get into the doghouse.

SECOND ACTOR (*to the* THIRD ACTOR): It no longer crowds him . . .

THIRD ACTOR: And he is in the doghouse.

SECOND ACTOR (*to the* FIRST ACTOR): Did you see how one can get used to anything?

ACTRESS: One gets used to anything . . .

SECOND AND THIRD ACTORS: Amen . . .

ACTRESS: And he did begin to get used to it.

THIRD ACTOR: Then, when you see someone come in, bark at me: bowwow . . . bowwow! Let's see . . .

FIRST ACTOR (*as the* SECOND ACTOR *runs past*): Bowwow . . . bowwow! (*The* SECOND ACTOR *passes by silently.*) Bowwow . . . wow . . . wow! (FIRST ACTOR *leaves.*)

THIRD ACTOR (*to the* SECOND ACTOR): It's ten pesos a day extra in our budget . . .

SECOND ACTOR: Hmmm!

THIRD ACTOR: . . . but the poor guy's so conscientious, he deserves them . . .

SECOND ACTOR: Hmmm!

THIRD ACTOR: Besides he doesn't eat any more than the dead one . . .

SECOND ACTOR: Hmmm!

THIRD ACTOR: We ought to help his family!

SECOND ACTOR: Hmmm! Hmmm! Hmmm!

(*They leave.*)

ACTRESS: Nevertheless, I found him very sad, and I tried to comfort him when he returned home. (*The* FIRST ACTOR *enters.*) We had visitors today! . . .

FIRST ACTOR: Really?

ACTRESS: The dances at the club, do you remember?

FIRST ACTOR: Yes.

ACTRESS: What was our tango?

FIRST ACTOR: I don't know.

ACTRESS: What do you mean, you don't know! "Love, you abandoned me. . . ." (*The* FIRST ACTOR *is on all fours.*) And one day you brought me a carnation. . . . (*She looks at him and is horrified.*) What are you doing?

FIRST ACTOR: What?

ACTRESS: You're on all fours . . . (*She leaves.*)

FIRST ACTOR: I can't bear this any more! I'm going to talk with the boss!

(*The* SECOND AND THIRD ACTORS *enter.*)

THIRD ACTOR: The fact is that there's nothing available . . .

FIRST ACTOR: They told me that an old man died.

THIRD ACTOR: Yes, but we're on an austerity budget. Wait a little more time, huh?

ACTRESS: And he waited. He returned in three months.

FIRST ACTOR (*to the* SECOND ACTOR): They told me that one guy retired . . .

SECOND ACTOR: Yes, but we intend to close that section. Wait a little more, huh?

ACTRESS: And he waited. He returned in two months.

FIRST ACTOR (*to the* THIRD ACTOR): Give me the job of one of the guys you fired because of the strike . . .

THIRD ACTOR: Impossible. Their positions will remain unfilled . . .

SECOND AND THIRD ACTORS: As punishment! (*They leave.*)

FIRST ACTOR: Then I couldn't take any more . . . and I quit!

ACTRESS: It was our happiest night in a long time. (*She takes him by the arm.*) What's the name of this flower?

FIRST ACTOR: Flower . . .

ACTRESS: And what's the name of that star?

FIRST ACTOR: Maria.

ACTRESS (*laughing*): Maria's my name!

FIRST ACTOR: The star's too, the star's too! (*He takes her hand and kisses it.*)

ACTRESS (*pulls back her hand*): Don't bite me!

FIRST ACTOR: I wasn't going to bite you. . . . I was going to kiss you, Maria . . .

ACTRESS: Ah! I thought that you were going to bite me. . . .

(*She leaves. The* SECOND AND THIRD ACTORS *enter.*)

SECOND ACTOR: Of course . . .

THIRD ACTOR: . . . and the next morning . . .

SECOND AND THIRD ACTORS: He had to look for a job again.

FIRST ACTOR: I went around to several places, until in one of them . . .

THIRD ACTOR: Look, . . . we don't have anything. Except . . .

FIRST ACTOR: Except what?

THIRD ACTOR: Last night the night watchman's dog died.

SECOND ACTOR: He was thirty-five, the poor wretch . . .

SECOND AND THIRD ACTORS: The poor wretch.

FIRST ACTOR: And I had to accept again.

SECOND ACTOR: We did pay him, fifteen pesos a day. (*The* SECOND AND THIRD ACTORS *walk back and forth.*) Hmmm! . . . Hmmm! . . . Hmmm! . . .

SECOND AND THIRD ACTORS: All right, let it be fifteen! (*They leave.*)

ACTRESS (*enters*): Of course the four hundred and fifty pesos won't be enough for us to pay the rent . . .

FIRST ACTOR: Look, since I have the doghouse, move to a room with four or five other girls, all right?

ACTRESS: There's no other solution. And since your salary isn't even enough for us to eat on . . .

FIRST ACTOR: Look, since I've gotten used to bones, I'm going to bring the meat to you, all right?

SECOND AND THIRD ACTORS (*entering*): The board of directors agreed!

FIRST ACTOR AND ACTRESS: The board of directors agreed . . . hurrah for the board of directors!

(SECOND AND THIRD ACTORS *leave*.)

FIRST ACTOR: I'd already gotten used to it. The doghouse seemed larger to me. Walking on all fours wasn't very different from walking upright. Maria and I would meet each other in the square. . . . (*He goes toward her.*) You can't come into my doghouse, and since I can't come into your room. . . . Until one night. . . .

ACTRESS: We were walking. And suddenly I felt sick . . .

FIRST ACTOR: What's the matter with you?

ACTRESS: I feel sick.

FIRST ACTOR: How come?

ACTRESS (*weeping*): I think . . . that I'm going to have a baby . . .

FIRST ACTOR: And that's why you're crying?

ACTRESS: I'm afraid . . . , I'm afraid!

FIRST ACTOR: But, why?

ACTRESS: I'm afraid . . . , I'm afraid! I don't want to have a baby!

FIRST ACTOR: Why, Maria? Why?

ACTRESS: I'm afraid . . . that it will be . . . (*She whispers.*) "a dog." (*The* FIRST ACTOR *looks at her terrified and leaves running and bark-*

ing. She falls to the floor. She gets up.) He left . . . , he left running!
Sometimes he'd stand up, and sometimes he'd run on all fours . . .

FIRST ACTOR: It isn't true, I didn't stand up. I couldn't stand up! My
back hurt me if I stood up! Bowwow! . . . Cars almost ran over
me . . . People stared at me . . . (*The* SECOND AND THIRD ACTORS *enter.*)
Go away! Didn't you ever see a dog?

SECOND ACTOR: He's mad! Call a doctor! (*He leaves.*)

THIRD ACTOR: He's drunk! Call a policeman! (*He leaves.*)

ACTRESS: Later they told me that a man had pity on him and approached him kindly.

SECOND ACTOR (*entering*): Do you feel sick, friend? You can't remain
on all fours. Do you know how many beautiful things there are to
see, standing up, with your eyes turned upward? Let's see, stand
up. . . . I'll help you. . . . Come on, stand up . . .

FIRST ACTOR (*beginning to stand up, when suddenly*): Bowwow . . .
bowwow! . . . (*He bites the* SECOND ACTOR.) Bowwow . . . bowwow!
. . . (*He leaves.*)

THIRD ACTOR (*entering*): Finally, when after two years without seeing him, we asked his wife, "How is he?" she answered . . .

ACTRESS: I don't know.

SECOND ACTOR: Is he all right?

ACTRESS: I don't know.

THIRD ACTOR: Is he sick?

ACTRESS: I don't know.

SECOND AND THIRD ACTORS: Where is he?

ACTRESS: In the dog pound.

THIRD ACTOR: And as we were coming here, a boxer passed by . . .

SECOND ACTOR: And they told us that he didn't know how to read, but that it didn't matter because he was a boxer.

THIRD ACTOR: And a draftee passed by . . .

ACTRESS: And a policeman passed by . . .

SECOND ACTOR: And they all passed by . . . , and they passed by . . . , and you passed by. And we thought that perhaps the story of our friend would matter to you.

ACTRESS: Because perhaps among you there may now be a woman who thinks: "Won't I have . . . , won't I have . . . ?" (She whispers.) "A dog."

THIRD ACTOR: Or someone who's been offered the job of the night watchman's dog . . .

ACTRESS: If it isn't so, we're happy.

SECOND ACTOR: But if it's so, if there is someone among you whom others want to change into a dog, like our friend, then . . . but well, then that . . . that's another story!

CURTAIN

✒ A Solid Home

Elena Garro

(Mexico)

Elena Garro

Both the theater and the dance held a particular appeal for Elena Garro from her earliest years. The Mexican dramatist, who was born December 11, 1920, in Puebla, devoted several years to the formal study of dancing. She also participated actively in the dance group at the Universidad Nacional Autónoma, from which she later received her degree. ■ Though Garro tried other genres, notably the narrative and biography, her principal contribution to Mexican letters lies in her theater. The presentation of three of her one-act pieces— *Andarse por las ramas, Los pilares de doña Blanca,* and *Un hogar sólido*—on the same program in 1957 marked her debut as a dramatist. At the same time, it brought a new creative voice to the Mexican stage. ■ Elena Garro has limited herself almost exclusively to the one-act play, a genre in which few can equal her artistic competence. In addition to the above plays, she has written *El encanto, tendajón mixto* (1858), *El Rey Mago* (1958), *Ventura Allende* (1958), *La señora en su balcón* (1966), *La mudanza* (1967), *Los perros* (1967), *El árbol* (1967), and three unpublished dramas—*La muerte de Felipe Ángeles, Parada empresa,* and *La dama boba.* ■ *Un hogar sólido,* the play presented here, explores life beyond the grave as the dead, together in the family tomb—with faint memories of this life and without yet having attained their promised paradise—ponder their status and the purpose of their existence; and is typical of this playwright's art. Garro's theater is a poetic one with echoes of oft-heard tales, children's games, and almost forgotten remembrances of little things. Deceptively simple, her theater deals with the more universal problems facing all men—loneliness, love, death, time.

A Solid Home

Characters

DON CLEMENT, sixty years old
DOÑA GERTRUDE, forty years old
MAMA JESSIE, eighty years old
KATIE, five years old
VINCENT MEJÍA, twenty-three years old
MUNI, twenty-eight years old
EVE, a foreigner, twenty years old
LYDIA, thirty-two years old

(*Interior of a small room with stone walls and ceiling. There are neither windows nor doors. To the left, imbedded in the wall and of stone also, are some berths. In one of them,* MAMA JESSIE *in a night-gown and a lace sleeping cap. The stage is very dark.*)

VOICE OF DOÑA GERTRUDE: Clement! Clement! I hear footsteps!

VOICE OF DON CLEMENT: You're always hearing footsteps! Why must women be so impatient? Always anticipating what isn't going to happen, predicting calamities!

VOICE OF DOÑA GERTRUDE: Well, I hear them.

VOICE OF DON CLEMENT: No, woman, you're always mistaken. You're carried away by your nostalgia for catastrophes. . . .

VOICE OF DOÑA GERTRUDE: It's true . . . but this time I'm not mistaken.

VOICE OF KATIE: They're many feet, Gertrude! (KATIE *comes out dressed in an ancient white dress, high black shoes, and a coral necklace. Her hair is tied at the nape of her neck with a red bow*). How nice! Now nice! Tra-la-la! Tra-la-la! (*She jumps and claps her hands.*)

37

DOÑA GERTRUDE (*appearing in a rose dress of the 1930s*): Children don't make mistakes. Aunt Katherine, isn't it true that someone is coming?

KATIE: Yes, I know it! I knew it from the first time that they came! I was so afraid here all alone. . . .

DON CLEMENT (*appearing in a black suit with white cuffs*): I believe that they're right. Gertrude! Gertrude! Help me find my metacarpuses. I always lose them and I can't shake hands without them.

VINCENT MEJÍA (*appearing in a uniform of an officer of Benito Juárez*): You read a lot, Don Clement, that's why you have the bad habit of forgetting things. Look at me, perfect in my uniform, always ready for any occasion!

MAMA JESSIE (*straightening up in her berth and poking out her head which is covered with the lace sleeping cap*): Katie's right! The steps are coming this way. (*She puts one hand behind her ear as though listening.*) The first ones have stopped . . . unless the Ramirezes have had a misfortune. . . . This neighborhood has already been very disappointing to us!

KATIE (*jumping*): You, go to sleep, Jessie! You only like to sleep:
Rock-a-bye Jessie,
on the tree top.
When the wind blows,
the cradle will rock.
When the bough bends,
the cradle will fall.
And down will come Jessie,
cradle and all.

MAMA JESSIE: And what do you want me to do? If they left me in my nightgown . . .

DON CLEMENT: Don't complain, Mama Jessie. We thought that out of respect . . .

DOÑA GERTRUDE: If it had been up to me, mama . . . , but what were the girls and Clement going to do?

(*Many footsteps which stop and then start again are heard overhead.*)

MAMA JESSIE: Katie! Come here and polish my forehead. I want it to shine like the North Star. Happy the day when I went through the house like lightning, sweeping, shaking the dust that would fall on the piano in deceptive gold mists. Then when everything shone like a comet, I'd break the ice on my buckets of water left out in the night air and bathe myself with water full of winter stars. Do you remember, Gertrude! That was living! Surrounded by my children straight and clean as lead pencils.

DOÑA GERTRUDE: Yes, mama. And I also remember the burnt cork you used to make circles under your eyes with, and the lemons you'd eat so that you'd look pale. And those nights when you would go with papa to the theater. How pretty you looked with your fan and your drop earrings!

MAMA JESSIE: You see, daughter, life is short. Each time that I would arrive at our box. . . .

DON CLEMENT (*interrupting*): For pity's sake, now I can't find my femur!

MAMA JESSIE: What a lack of courtesy! To interrupt a lady!

(*Meanwhile,* KATIE *has been helping* JESSIE *arrange her nightcap.*)

VINCENT MEJÍA: I saw Katie using it for a trumpet.

DOÑA GERTRUDE: Aunt Katie, where did you leave Clement's femur?

KATIE: Jessie, Jessie! They want to take my bugle away from me!

MAMA JESSIE: Gertrude, let this child alone! And as for you, let me tell you for a grown woman you're more spoiled than she is. . . .

DOÑA GERTRUDE: But, mama, don't be unjust. It's Clement's femur!

KATIE: Ugly! Bad! I'll hit you! It's not his femur, it's my little sugar bugle!

DON CLEMENT (*to* GERTRUDE): Could she have eaten it? Your aunt's unbearable.

DOÑA GERTRUDE: I don't know, Clement. My broken clavicle got lost. She liked the little streaks left along the scar a lot. And it was my favorite bone! It reminded me of the walls of my house, covered with heliotrope. I told you how I fell, didn't I? The day before, we'd gone to the circus. All of Chihuahua was in the stands to see the clown, Richard Bell. Suddenly a tightrope walker came out. She resembled a butterfly. I've never forgotten her. . . . (*A blow is heard above.* GERTRUDE *interrupts herself. Continuing:*) In the morning I climbed the fence to dance on one foot, because all night I'd dreamed that I was she. . . . (*Overhead a harder blow is heard.*) Of course, I didn't know that I had bones. As a little girl, one doesn't know anything. Because I broke it, I always say that it was the first little bone that I had. It takes you by surprise!

(*The blows follow one another more rapidly.*)

VINCENT MEJÍA (*smoothing his mustache*): There's no doubt. Someone's coming. We have guests. (*He sings.*)
　　　　When in darkness
　　　　The moon glimmers
　　　　And on the pool
　　　　The swallow sings . . .

MAMA JESSIE: Be quiet, Vincent! This isn't the time to sing. Look at these unexpected guests! In my day people announced themselves before dropping in for a visit. There was more respect. Let's see now whom they're bringing us, probably one of those foreigners who married my girls! "God overwhelms the humble!" as my poor Raymond, may God have him in His glory, used to say. . . .

VINCENT MEJÍA: You haven't improved at all, Jessie! You find defects in everything. Before, you were so agreeable. The only thing you liked was to dance polkas! (*He hums a tune and dances a few steps.*) Do you remember how we danced at that carnival? (*He continues dancing.*) Your pink dress spun around and around, and your neck was very close to my lips . . .

MAMA JESSIE: For heaven's sake, cousin Vincent! Don't remind me of those foolish things.

VINCENT MEJÍA (*laughing*): What would Raymond say now? He was so jealous. And you and I here together, while he rots there alone in that other cemetery.

DOÑA GERTRUDE: Uncle Vincent, be quiet. You're going to cause an argument!

DON CLEMENT (*alarmed*): I already explained to you, Mama Jessie, that at the time we didn't have the money to transfer him.

MAMA JESSIE: And the girls, why don't they bring him? Don't give me explanations. You always lacked tact.

(*A harder blow is heard.*)

KATIE: I saw a light! (*A ray of light enters.*) I saw a sword. St. Michael's coming to visit us again! Look at his sword!

VINCENT MEJÍA: Are we all here? Now then, easy does it!

DON CLEMENT: Muni and my sister-in-law are missing.

MAMA JESSIE: The foreigners, always keeping away!

DOÑA GERTRUDE: Muni, Muni! Someone's coming. Maybe it's one of your cousins. Aren't you happy, dear? You'll be able to play and laugh with them again. Let's see if that sadness leaves you.

(*EVE appears, blond, tall, sad, very young, in a traveling dress of the 1920s.*)

EVE: Muni was around here a moment ago. Muni, dear! Do you hear that blow? That's the way the sea beats against the rocks of my house. . . . None of you knew it. . . . It was a rock, high, like a wave, always beaten by the winds that lulled us to sleep at night. Swirls of salt covered its windows with sea stars. The walls in the kitchen had a golden glow which radiated from my father's hands, warm as the sun. . . . During the nights, creatures of wind, water, fire, and salt came in through the fireplace. They would huddle in the flames and sing in the water that dripped into the washstands. . . . Drip! Drop! Drip! Drop! Drip! Drop! . . . And iodine spread itself about the house like sleep. . . . The tail of a shining dolphin would announce day to us, with this light of fish scales and corals!

(*With the last sentence,* EVE *raises her arm and points to the torrent of light that enters the crypt when the first stone slab is moved above. The room is inundated with sunlight. All the luxurious clothes are dusty and all the faces pale. The child* KATIE *jumps with pleasure.*)

KATIE: Look, Jessie! Someone's coming! Who's bringing him, Jessie? Lady Diptheria or Saint Michael?

MAMA JESSIE: Wait, child. We're going to see.

KATIE: Lady Diptheria brought me. Do you remember her? She had fingers of cotton and she wouldn't let me breathe. Did she frighten you, Jessie?

MAMA JESSIE: Yes, little sister. I remember that they took you away and the patio of the house remained strewn with purple petals. Mama cried a lot and we girls did too.

KATIE: Dummy! Didn't you know that you were going to come to play with me here? That day, St. Michael sat down beside me and wrote it with his sword of fire on the roof of my house. I didn't know how to read . . . and I read it. And was the school of the Misses Simson nice?

MAMA JESSIE: Very nice, Katie. Mama sent us with black ribbons . . . .

KATIE: And did you learn to spell? That's why mama was going to send me. . . .

MUNI (*comes in wearing pajamas, with a blue face and blond hair*): Who can it be?

(*Overhead, through the fragment of the vault open to the sky, a woman's feet are seen suspended in a circle of light.*)

DOÑA GERTRUDE: Clement, Clement! They're Lydia's feet. What a pleasure, daughter, what a pleasure that you've died so soon!

(*Everyone becomes silent. The descent of* LYDIA, *suspended on ropes, begins. She is stiff, wearing a white dress, her arms crossed on her chest, her fingers in the form of a cross, and her head bowed. Her eyes are closed.*)

KATIE: Who's Lydia?

MUNI: Lydia's the daughter of my uncle Clement and my aunt Gertrude, Katie. (*He caresses the girl.*)

MAMA JESSIE: Now we have the whole bunch of grandchildren here. So many brats! Well, isn't the crematory oven more modern? As far as I'm concerned at least it seems more hygienic.

KATIE: Isn't it true, Jessie, that Lydia isn't for real?

MAMA JESSIE: I wish it were so, my dear. There's room here for everyone except my poor Raymond!

EVE: How she grew! When I came she was as little as Muni.

(LYDIA *remains standing, in the midst of all of them, as they look at her. Then she opens her eyes and sees them.*)

LYDIA: Papa! (*She embraces him.*) Mama! Muni! (*She embraces them.*)

DOÑA GERTRUDE: You're looking very well, daughter.

LYDIA: And grandmother?

DON CLEMENT: She can't get up. Do you remember that we made the mistake of burying her in her nightgown?

MAMA JESSIE: Yes, Lili, here I am, lying down forever.

DOÑA GERTRUDE: My mother's notions! You already know, Lili, how well groomed she always was.

MAMA JESSIE: The worst thing will be, daughter, to present myself this way before God, our Lord. Doesn't it seem a disgrace to you? Why didn't it occur to you to bring me a dress? That gray one with the brocade ruffles and the bouquet of violets at the neck. Do you remember it? I'd put it on for formal occasions . . . but no one remembers the old people. . . .

KATIE: When Saint Michael visits us, she hides.

LYDIA: And who are you, precious?

KATIE: Katie!

LYDIA: Of course! We had your picture on the piano! Now it's in Evie's house. How sad it was to look at you, so melancholy, painted in your white dress. I'd forgotten that you were here.

VINCENT MEJÍA: And aren't you pleased to meet me, niece?

LYDIA: Uncle Vincent! We also had your picture in the living room, with your uniform and your medal in a little red velvet box.

EVE: And don't you remember your Aunt Eve?

LYDIA: Aunt Eve! Yes, I just barely remember you, with your blond hair spread out in the sun . . . and I remember your purple parasol and your faded face under it, like that of a beautiful drowned woman . . . and your empty chair rocking to the rhythm of your song, after you had gone.

(*From the circle of light a* VOICE *comes forth.*)

VOICE: The generous earth of our Mexico opens its arms to give you loving shelter. Virtuous woman, most exemplary mother, model wife, you leave an irreparable void . . .

MAMA JESSIE: Who's speaking to you with such familiarity?

LYDIA: It's Don Gregory de la Huerta Ramírez Puente, President of the Association of the Blind.

VINCENT MAJÍA: What madness! And what do so many blind people do together?

MAMA JESSIE: But why does he address you in such intimate terms?

DOÑA GERTRUDE: It's the style, mama, to address the dead familiarly.

VOICE: Most cruel loss, whose absence we shall feel in time. You leave us forever deprived of your boundless charm. You also leave a solid and Christian home in the most terrible neglect. The homes do tremble before inexorable Death. . . .

DON CLEMENT: Good God! But is that blustering fool still running around there?

MAMA JESSIE: What's useless abounds.

LYDIA: Yes, and now he's president of the bank, of the Knights of Columbus, of the Association for the Blind, the Flag Day and Mother's Day Committees.

VOICE: Only irrevocable faith, Christian resignation, and pity . . .

KATIE: Don Hilary always says the same thing.

MAMA JESSIE: It isn't Don Hilary, Katie. Don Hilary died a trifling sixty-five years ago. . . .

KATIE (not hearing her): When they brought me, he said, "A little angel flew away!" And it wasn't true. I was here below, alone and very frightened. Isn't that so Vincent? Isn't it true that I don't tell lies?

VINCENT MEJÍA: You're telling me! Imagine, I arrived here, still stunned by the powder flashes, with my wounds open . . . and what do I see? Katie crying: "I want to see my mama! I want to see my mama!" What trouble she caused me! Believe me, I'd rather have fought the French. . . .

VOICE: Rest in peace!

(*They begin to replace the stone slabs. The scene becomes dark slowly.*)

KATIE: We were alone a long time, weren't we, Vincent? We didn't know what was happening, but no one came anymore.

MAMA JESSIE: I've already told you, Katie, we went to the capital, then the revolution came along. . . .

KATIE: Until one day Eve arrived. You said, Vincent, that she was a foreigner. . . .

VINCENT MEJÍA: The situation was a little tense and Eve didn't say a single word to us.

EVE: I too was restrained . . . and besides I was thinking of Muni . . . and of my home. . . . Everything was so quiet here.

(*Silence. They place the last slab.*)

LYDIA: And now, what'll we do?

DON CLEMENT: Wait.

LYDIA: Still wait?

DOÑA GERTRUDE: Yes, daughter. You'll see.

EVE: You'll see everything you want to see, except your home with your white pine table and the waves and the sails of the boats through your windows.

MUNI: Aren't you happy, Lili?

LYDIA: Yes, Muni, especially to see you. When I saw you that night lying in the courtyard of the police station, with that smell of urine that came from the broken flagstones, and you dead on the stretcher, between the feet of the policemen with your wrinkled pajamas and your blue face, I asked myself, "Why? Why?"

KATIE: Me too, Lili. I hadn't seen a blue dead person either. Then Jessie told me that cyanide has many artists' brushes, but only one tube of color, blue!

MAMA JESSIE: Don't bother that boy any longer! Blue looks very good on blonds.

MUNI: Why, cousin Lili? Haven't you seen stray dogs walk and walk along the sidewalks looking for bones in the butcher shops full of flies, and the butcher, with his fingers drenched in blood from cutting up the meat? Well, I no longer wanted to walk along atrocious sidewalks looking through the blood for a bone, nor look at those corners, shelters for drunks and urinals for dogs. I wanted a happy city, full of sunlight and moonlight. A solid city like the home we had as children, with sunshine in every door, moonlight for every window, and wandering stars in the rooms. Do you remember it, Lili? It had a labyrinth of laughs. Its kitchen was a crossroads; its garden, source of all the rivers; and all of it, the birthplace of Man. . . .

LYDIA: A solid home, Muni! That's just what I wanted . . . and you already know, they took me to a strange house. And in it I found only clocks and eyes without eyelids that looked at me for years. . . . I polished the floors so as not to see the thousands of dead words that the maids swept in the mornings. I shined the mirrors in order to drive away our hostile glances. I hoped that one morning the loving image would face me in the looking glass. I opened books in order to open avenues in that circular hell. I embroidered napkins with linked initials in order to find the magic, unbreakable thread that made two names into one. . . .

MUNI: I know, Lili.

LYDIA: But it was all useless. The furious eyes didn't stop looking at me ever. If I could find the spider that once lived in my house— I used to tell myself—with the invisible thread that unites the flower to light, the apple to fragrance, woman to man, I would sew loving eyelids to close the eyes that look at me and this house would enter

into the solar order. Each balcony would be a different country.
Its furniture would bloom. From its glasses jets of water would spurt.
The sheets would turn into magic carpets in order to travel to sleep.
From the hands of my children, castles, flags, and battles would come
forth . . . but I didn't find the thread, Muni. . . .

MUNI: You told me that at the police station. In that strange courtyard, forever far from the other courtyard, in whose sky a belltower
counted for us the hours that we had left to play.

LYDIA: Yes, Muni, and with you I put away forever the last day that
we were children. Afterward, only a Lydia seated, facing the wall,
waiting, remained.

MUNI: I couldn't grow, either, and live on the street corners. I wanted
my home. . . .

EVE: Me too, Muni, my son, I wanted a solid home. A house that
the sea would beat every night. Boom! Boom! A house that would
laugh with my father's laugh full of fish and nets.

MUNI: Don't be sad, Lili. You'll find the thread, and you'll find the
spider.

DON CLEMENT: Lili, aren't you happy? Now your house is the center
of the sun, the heart of every star, the root of all the grasses, the
most solid point of every stone.

MUNI: Yes, Lili, you still don't know it, but suddenly you won't
need a house, nor a river. We'll not swim in the Mezcala River,
we'll be the Mezcala.

DOÑA GERTRUDE: At times, daughter, you'll be very cold, and you'll
be the snow falling on an unknown city or gray roofs and red caps.

KATIE: What I like most is being a piece of candy in a little girl's
mouth. Or a sty, to make those who read near a window weep!

MUNI: Don't grieve when your eyes begin to disappear, because
then you'll be all the eyes of the dogs looking at absurd feet.

MAMA JESSIE: Ah, child! May you never be the eyes of the blind, of a blind fish in the deepest abyss of the seas! You don't know the terrible feeling that I had. It was like seeing and not seeing things never thought of.

KATIE (*laughing and clapping*): You also were very frightened when you were the worm that came in and out of your mouth.

VINCENT MEJÍA: Well, for me, the worst thing was being a murderer's dagger!

MAMA JESSIE: Now the gophers will return. Don't shout when you yourself run along your face.

DON CLEMENT: Don't tell her that. You're going to frighten her. It's frightening to learn to be everything.

DOÑA GERTRUDE: Especially because in the world one scarcely learns to be a man.

LYDIA: And will I be able to be a pine tree with a nest of spiders and build a solid home?

DON CLEMENT: Of course! And you'll be the pine tree and the staircase and the fire.

LYDIA: And then?

MAMA JESSIE: Then God will call us to his bosom.

DON CLEMENT: After having learned to be all things, St. Michael's sword will appear, center of the universe, and by its light the divine armies of angels will come forth and we'll enter into the celestial order.

MUNI: I want to be the fold of an angel's tunic.

MAMA JESSIE: Your color will go very well. It'll give beautiful reflections. And I, what'll I do dressed in this nightgown?

KATIE: I want to be the index finger of God the Father!

ALL TOGETHER: Child!

EVE: And I, a wave sprinkled with salt, changed into a cloud!

LYDIA: And I the sewing fingers of the Virgin, embroidering . . . embroidering . . . !

DOÑA GERTRUDE: And I the music from the harp of St. Cecilia!

VINCENT MEJÍA: And I the rage of the sword of St. Gabriel!

DON CLEMENT: And I a particle of the stone of St. Peter!

KATIE: And I a window that looks at the world!

MAMA JESSIE: There'll no longer be a world, Katie, because we'll be all that after the Final Judgment.

KATIE (*weeping*): There'll no longer be a world. And when am I going to see it? I didn't see anything. I didn't even learn the spelling book. I want there to be a world.

VINCENT MEJÍA: Look at it now, Katie!

(*In the distance a trumpet is heard.*)

MAMA JESSIE: Jesus, Mary Most Pure! The trumpet of Final Judgment! And me in a nightgown! Pardon me, my Lord, this immodesty!

LYDIA: No, grandma, it's taps. There's a barracks near the cemetery.

MAMA JESSIE: Ah, yes, they had already told me! And I always forget it. Who had the bright idea of putting a barracks so close to us? What a government! It lends itself to so much confusion!

VINCENT MEJÍA: Taps! I'm going. I'm the wind that opens all the doors that I didn't open, that goes up the stairs that I never went up in a whirl, that runs along new streets in my officer's uniform and lifts the skirts of the pretty, unknown girls. . . . Ah, coolness! (*He disappears.*)

MAMA JESSIE: Rascal!

DON CLEMENT: Ah, rain on the water! (*He disappears.*)

DOÑA GERTRUDE: Wood in flames! (*She disappears.*)

MUNI: Do you hear? A dog howls. Ah, melancholy! (*He disappears.*)

KATIE: The table where nine children eat supper! I'm the game they play! (*She disappears.*)

MAMA JESSIE: The fresh heart of a head of lettuce! (*She disappears.*)

EVE: I'm the flash of fire that sinks into the black sea! (*She disappears.*)

LYDIA: A solid home! That's what I am! The stone slabs of my tomb! (*She disappears.*)

CURTAIN

Crossroads

Carlos Solórzano

(Guatemala)

Carlos Solórzano

Born in San Marcos, Guatemala, in 1922, Carlos Solórzano moved at sixteen to Mexico, where he has since made his home. He earned a degree in architecture in 1944 and a doctorate in literature in 1948—both from the Universidad Nacional Autónoma. He pursued additional study of the theater in France and Italy as well as in the United States. At different times he has taught as a visiting professor in universities in this country. In 1959 he founded the Teatro Universitario Profesional and the Teatro Estudiantil Universitario. He has represented Mexico at various international seminars on the theater. ■ At present Solórzano is a professor in the Facultad de Filosofía y Letras of the Universidad Nacional Autónoma and director of its Departamento de Literatura Hispanoamericana. He also serves as director of the Museo Nacional de Teatro. ■ The Guatemalan playwright has freely acknowledged his debt to Albert Camus and Michel de Ghelderode, calling them his "great friends and teachers." Solórzano has described his drama as one in which the characters find themselves "wooed by two contradictory forces that live within the same human temperament: submission and rebelliousness in a struggle to attain liberty. Liberty [it is understood] that extends to all orders of existence."[1] He avails himself of different techniques in his works, which include *Doña Beatriz* (1950), *La muerte hizo la luz* (1951), *El hechicero* (1954), *Las manos de Dios* (1956), *El crucificado* (1957), *Cruce de vías, Los fantoches, Mea culpa* (1958), *El sueño del ángel* (1960), and *El zapato* (1965). ■ Though written in 1958, *Crossroads* (*Cruce de vías*) was not staged until 1966. It appeared in Mexico as part of a double bill with Solórzano's translation from the French of Ghelderode's *School of Buffoons*. This one-act play, set in a symbolic railroad station, makes a telling observation on the anguish man all too often suffers because of a self-imposed blindness. ■ As a critic, anthologist, scholar, and dramatist, Carlos Solórzano has contributed immeasurably to the resurgence of the contemporary theater in Latin America.

1. Carlos Solórzano, ed., *Teatro guatemalteco* (Madrid: Aguilar, 1964), p. 26.

Crossroads

A Sad Vaudeville

Characters

THE FLAGMAN
THE TRAIN
THE MAN
THE WOMAN

Setting: Stage empty, dark. At one end, a semaphore that alternately flashes a green light and a red one. In the center, hang-
ing from the ceiling, a big clock whose hands show five o'clock
sharp.

(*The characters will move mechanically, like characters in the silent
movies. The* MAN *in fast motion; the* WOMAN, *in slow motion. As
the curtain rises, the* FLAGMAN *is at the end of the stage, opposite the
semaphore, with a lighted lantern in his hand. He is standing very
stiffly and indifferently.*)

FLAGMAN (*staring into space, in an impersonal voice*): The trains
from the North travel toward the South, the trains from the North
travel toward the South, the trains from the North travel toward the
South. (*He repeats the refrain several times while The* TRAIN *crosses
the back of the stage. The* TRAIN *will be formed by three men dressed
in gray. As they pass by, they each mechanically perform a pantomime with one arm extended, the hand on the shoulder of the man in
front, and the other arm making a circular motion, synchronized
with the rhythm of the* FLAGMAN's *words.*) The trains from the North
travel toward the South (*etc.*). (*Loud train whistle. The* MAN *who
comes at the end of the* TRAIN *breaks free of it by making a movement as though he were jumping off. The* TRAIN *disappears on the
right.*)

MAN (*carrying a small valise. He glances around the place, then looks at the clock, which he compares with his watch. He is young, serene of face, approximately twenty-five years old. He addresses the* FLAGMAN): Good afternoon. (*As a reply, he receives the latter's refrain.*) Is this the place this ticket indicates? (*He places it in front of the* FLAGMAN's *eyes. The* FLAGMAN *nods.*) A train stops here, just about now, doesn't it?

FLAGMAN (*without looking at him*): Trains never stop here.

MAN: Are you the flagman?

FLAGMAN: They call me by many names.

MAN: Then, perhaps you've seen a woman around here.

FLAGMAN: I've seen no one.

MAN (*approaching him*): Do you know? The woman I'm looking for is . . .

FLAGMAN (*interrupting*): They all look alike.

MAN: Oh, no! She's different. She's the woman that I've been waiting for for many years. She'll be wearing a white flower on her dress. Or is it yellow? (*He searches nervously in his pockets and takes out a paper that he reads.*) No, it's white . . . that's what she says in her letter. (*The* FLAGMAN *takes a few steps, feeling ill at ease.*) Pardon me for telling you all this, but now you'll be able to understand how important it is for me to find this woman, because . . .

FLAGMAN (*interrupting again*): What woman?

MAN: The one that I'm looking for.

FLAGMAN: I don't know what woman you're looking for.

MAN: The one that I've just told you about.

FLAGMAN: Ah. . . .

MAN: Perhaps she has passed by and you didn't see her. (*The* FLAG-

MAN *shrugs his shoulders*.) Well, I guess that I have to tell you everything to see if you can remember. She's tall, slender, with black hair and big blue eyes. She's wearing a white flower on her dress. . . . (*Anxiously*.) Hasn't she been around here?

FLAGMAN: I can't know if someone I don't know has been around.

MAN: Excuse me. I know that I'm nervous but I have the impression that we aren't speaking the same language, that is, that you aren't answering my questions. . . .

FLAGMAN: That's not my job.

MAN: Nevertheless, I believe that a flagman ought to know how to answer questions. (*Transition*.) She wrote to me that she'd be here at five, at the railroad crossing of . . . (*He reads the ticket*.) I'll never know how to pronounce this name, but I know that it's here. We chose this point because it's halfway between our homes. Even for this kind of date, a romantic one, one must be fair. (*The* FLAGMAN *looks at him without understanding*.) Yes, romantic. (*With ingenuous pride:*) Maybe I'll bore you, but I must tell you that one day I saw an ad in a magazine. It was hers. How well written that ad was! She said that she needed a young man like me, to establish relations with so as not to live so alone. (*Pause*.) I wrote to her and she answered me. Then I sent her my photo and she sent me hers. You can't imagine what a beauty!

FLAGMAN (*who has not heard most of the account*): Is she selling something?

MAN (*surprised*): Who?

FLAGMAN: The woman who placed the ad.

MAN: No, for heaven's sake! She placed that ad because she said that she was shy, and she thought it might help and . . .

FLAGMAN: Everyone sells something.

MAN (*impatiently*): You just don't understand me.

FLAGMAN: It's possible. . . .

MAN: Well, I mean . . . understand how excited I am on coming to meet someone whom I don't know but who . . .

FLAGMAN: How's that?

MAN (*upset*): That is, I know her well, but I haven't seen her.

FLAGMAN: That's very common.

MAN: Do you think so?

FLAGMAN: The contrary's also common.

MAN: I don't understand.

FLAGMAN: It isn't necessary.

MAN: But you only speak nonsense! I should warn you that although I've an inclination toward romantic things, I'm a man who isn't pleased by jokes in bad taste. (*The* FLAGMAN *shrugs his shoulders again.*) Besides, this delay upsets me as does this dark place with that clock that doesn't run. It seems like a timeless place.

(*Suddenly a loud train whistle is heard. The semaphore comes to life flashing the green light. The* FLAGMAN *again adopts his rigid posture, staring into space, he repeats his refrain.*)

FLAGMAN (*loudly*): The trains from the South travel toward the North. The trains from the South travel toward the North. The trains from the South travel toward the North (*etc.*).

(*The* TRAIN *passes across the back of the stage, from right to left.*)

MAN (*shouting*): There, on that train! . . . She should be on it. (*He rushes to meet the* TRAIN *which passes by without stopping, almost knocking him down. The* MAN *remains at stage center, his arms at his sides. Disillusioned:*) She wasn't on it.

FLAGMAN: It's only natural.

MAN: What do you mean?

FLAGMAN: He's never coming. . . .

MAN: Who?

FLAGMAN: The man we're waiting for.

MAN: But it's a question of a woman.

FLAGMAN: It's the same.

MAN: How is a man going to be the same as a woman?

FLAGMAN: He isn't the same, but in a certain way he is.

MAN: You change your mind quickly.

FLAGMAN: I don't know.

MAN (*furiously*): Then, what is it that you do know?

FLAGMAN (*indifferently*): Where they're going.

MAN: The trains?

FLAGMAN: They all go to the same place.

MAN: What do you mean?

FLAGMAN: They come and go, but they end by meeting one another. . . .

MAN: That would be impossible.

FLAGMAN: But it's true. The impossible is always true.

MAN (*as if these last words brought him back to reality, he abandons his furious attitude and calms down*): You're right in what you say. (*Hesitating.*) For example, my meeting with that woman seems impossible and it's the only certain thing of my whole existence. (*Suddenly, with an unexpected tone of anguish:*) But it's five ten. (*He looks at his watch.*) And she isn't coming. (*He takes the arm of the*

FLAGMAN *who remains indifferent.*) Help me, do all that is possible to remember! I'm sure that if you want to, you can tell me if you saw her or not. . . .

FLAGMAN: One can't know by just seeing a person whether it was the one who placed an ad in the newspaper.

MAN (*once again containing his ill humor*): But I already described what she's like to you! . . .

FLAGMAN (*imperturbably*): I'm sorry. I forgot. . . .

(*Meanwhile a* WOMAN *dressed in black has come in behind the* MAN. *She is tall and slim. Her face is covered by a heavy veil. She walks softly with a pantomime motion. On her dress she wears a very large white flower. On seeing her the* FLAGMAN *raises his lantern and examines her. The* MAN, *blinded by the light, covers his eyes. On seeing herself discovered, the* WOMAN *tears the white flower violently from her dress. She puts it in her purse and turns her back, remaining motionless.*)

MAN (*still covering his eyes*): Ooh! You're going to blind me with that lantern.

FLAGMAN (*returning to his habitual stiffness*): I beg your pardon. . . .

MAN (*to the* FLAGMAN): Someone has come in, right?

FLAGMAN: It's not important.

MAN (*recovering from the glare, he notices the presence of the* WOMAN *and runs toward her. He stops suddenly*): Ah . . . (*Timidly*) I beg you to. . . .

WOMAN (*her back turned*): Yes?

MAN (*embarrassed*): I thought that you . . . were someone . . .

WOMAN: Yes . . .

MAN (*with determination*): Someone I'm looking for. (*She does not move. Pause.*) Will you permit me to see you from the front?

WOMAN: From the front?

MAN (*upset*): Yes . . . it's absolutely necessary that I see you . . .

WOMAN (*without turning*): But . . . why? (*She begins to turn slowly.*)

MAN: Well . . . in order to . . . (*On seeing that her face is covered, he backs away.*) You aren't wearing anything on your dress . . . and nevertheless . . .

WOMAN (*trembling*): And nevertheless?

MAN: You have the same stature and build. . . .

WOMAN (*with a jesting tone*): Really?

MAN (*with distrust*): Could you tell me how you got here? I didn't see a train.

WOMAN (*interrupting, stammering*): I arrived . . . ahead of time . . . and I waited.

MAN: Ahead of what time?

WOMAN: We all wait for a time. Aren't you waiting for it?

MAN (*sadly*): Yes.

WOMAN: I believe that there is but one moment to recognize one another, to extend our hands. One musn't let it pass by.

MAN: What do you mean by that? Who are you?

WOMAN: Now I'm the woman I've always wanted to be.

MAN (*timidly*): Will you let me see your face?

WOMAN (*frightened*): Why?

MAN: I need to find that one face, the special one, the different one.

WOMAN (*moving away*): I am sorry. I can't.

MAN (*following her with a tortured motion*): Excuse me. I'm stupid, I know. For a moment I thought that you could be she. But it's absurd. If it were so, you'd come straight to me, for we have called one another from afar.

WOMAN (*trembling*): Perhaps she's more afraid of finding the one she seeks than of letting him pass by without stopping.

MAN: No, that would also be absurd. (*Transition.*) In any case, I beg your pardon. (*He moves away and sits down on his small suitcase, his back to the* WOMAN.) I'll wait here.

(*In the meantime, while the* MAN *is not looking at her, the* WOMAN *has raised her veil with long slow movements. When she uncovers her face, it is obvious that she is old. Her forehead is furrowed by deep wrinkles. She is like the mask of old age. This face contrasts obviously with her body, still slender, ageless.*)

WOMAN (*to the* FLAGMAN *who stares at her*): You saw me from the beginning, didn't you? Why didn't you tell him?

FLAGMAN (*indifferently*): Whom?

WOMAN (*pointing to the* MAN): Him, the only one.

FLAGMAN: I'd forgotten him.

WOMAN (*in a surge of anguish*): Shall I tell him that I'm that woman he's waiting for? Will he recognize in this old face the unsatisfied longing still in this body of mine? How can I tell him that I need him even more than when I was young, as young as I am in that touched-up photo that he's looking at?

(*In the meantime, the* MAN *studies the photograph with fascination. The* WOMAN *covers her face again with the veil and goes up to the* MAN.)

WOMAN: Is she very late?

MAN (*his back turned*): Of course. . . .

WOMAN: It would hurt you a great deal if she wouldn't come!

MAN (*turning forcefully*): She has to come.

WOMAN: Nevertheless, you must realize that perhaps she's afraid to reveal herself, that maybe she's waiting for you to discover her.

MAN: I don't understand.

WOMAN (*very close to the* MAN): I have a friend . . . who always lived alone, thinking nevertheless that the best thing for her was to get together with someone. (*She pauses. The* MAN *listens to her, interested.*) She was ugly, very ugly, perhaps that was why she dreamed of a man instead of looking for him. She liked to have her pictures taken. She had the photographs touched up, so that the picture turned out to be hers, but at the same time it was someone else's. She used to write to young men, sending them her photograph. She called them close to her house, with loving words. . . . When they arrived, she'd wait behind the windows; she wouldn't let herself be seen. . . .

MAN: Why are you telling me all this?

WOMAN (*without hearing*): She'd see them. She knew that they were there on account of her. Each day, a different one. She accumulated many memories, the faces, the bodies of those strong men who had waited for her.

MAN: How absurd! I think. . . .

WOMAN: You're also strong and young.

MAN (*confused*): Yes, but . . .

WOMAN: And today she's one day older than yesterday.

MAN (*after allowing a pause*): Really I don't see what relation all this can have to . . .

WOMAN (*drawing near and placing her hand on the* MAN's *head*): Perhaps you'll understand now. Close your eyes. (*She passes her hand over the eyes of the* MAN *in a loving manner.*) Have you never felt fear?

MAN: Fear? Of what?

WOMAN: Of living, of being . . . as if all your life you'd been waiting for something that never comes?

MAN: No. . . . (*He opens his eyes.*)

WOMAN: Tell me the truth. Close your eyes, those eyes that are separating us now. Have you been afraid?

(*The* MAN *closes his eyes.*)

MAN (*hesitatingly*): Well, a little. . . .

WOMAN (*with an absent voice*): A suffering . . . in solitude . . .

MAN: Yes, at times. . . . (*He takes the* WOMAN's *hand.*)

WOMAN: Above all when you begin to fall asleep. The solitude of your body, a body alone, that inevitably ages.

MAN: Yes, but . . .

WOMAN: The solitude of the heart that tries hard every night to prolong its cry against silence.

MAN: I've felt something like that . . . but . . . not so clearly . . . not so pointedly.

WOMAN: It's that . . . perhaps you were waiting for that voice, the one of someone invented by you, to your measure. . . .

MAN: Yes . . . I think that's it.

WOMAN: Would you be able to recognize that voice with your eyes open?

MAN: I'm sure that I could. . . .

WOMAN: Even if it were a voice invented many years before, in the dark inmost recesses of time?

MAN: It wouldn't matter. I'd know how to recognize it.

WOMAN: Then, is that what you're waiting for?

MAN: Yes. I'm here for her sake, looking for her.

WOMAN: She's waiting for you also. (*The* WOMAN *raises the veil little by little until she leaves her withered face in the open.*) She'll be only a memory for you, if you don't allow yourself to be overcome by time. Time is her worst enemy. Will you fight it?

(*They are seated very close to one another.*)

MAN: Yes.

WOMAN: All right. . . . Open your eyes.

(*The* MAN *opens his eyes slowly and is surprised to find himself held by the* WOMAN's *two hands. He stands up with a brusque movement.*)

MAN (*bewildered*): Excuse me, I'm confused . . .

WOMAN (*entreatingly*): Oh, no! . . . Don't tell me that . . .

MAN: It was a stupidity of mine . . .

WOMAN (*imploringly*): But you said . . .

MAN: It's ridiculous! For a moment I thought that you were she. Understand me. It was a wild dream . . .

WOMAN (*grieved*): Yes, yes . . .

MAN: I don't know how I could . . .

WOMAN (*calming herself*): I understand you. A wild dream and nothing more . . .

MAN: You're really very kind to pardon me. . . . (*Looking at his watch, astonished:*) It's five thirty! . . . (*Pause.*)

WOMAN (*sadly*): Yes. . . . Now I believe that she won't come.

MAN: How would that be possible?

WOMAN: It's better that way.

MAN: Who are you to tell me that?

WOMAN: No one. (*She opens her purse.*) Do you want this white flower?

MAN (*snatching it from her*): Where did you get it? Why are you giving it to me?

WOMAN: I picked it up . . . in passing . . .

MAN (*with great excitement*): But then, she has been here. Perhaps she has gotten lost or mistaken the place. Or perhaps, while I was here talking with you, she has passed by without stopping.

WOMAN (*covering her face*): I already told you that there is but a moment to recognize oneself, to close one's eyes . . .

MAN: But now . . . what can I do in order to . . . find her?

WOMAN: Wait . . . as everyone does. . . . Wait . . . (*She takes the flower again.*)

MAN: But, what about you?

WOMAN: I'll continue searching, calling them, seeing them pass by. When you're old, you'll understand. (*The train whistle is heard. The* WOMAN *moves away from the* MAN, *with sorrowful movements.*) Good-bye, good-bye . . .

MAN (*to himself*): Who can this woman be who speaks to me as if she knew me? (*He runs toward her. He checks himself.*) Good-bye . . .

(*The semaphore flashes the green light. The* FLAGMAN *becomes stiff in order to repeat his refrain.*)

FLAGMAN: The trains from the North travel toward the South, the trains from the North travel toward the South, the trains from the

North travel toward the South, the trains from the North travel toward the South (*etc.*).

(*The* TRAIN *crosses the back of the stage. The* WOMAN *waves the flower sadly and with long movements approaches the* TRAIN. *She gets on it. The* FLAGMAN *repeats his refrain while the* TRAIN *leaves dragging the* WOMAN, *who goes off with writhing and anguished pantomime movements.*)

MAN (*with a certain sadness, to the* FLAGMAN *who remains indifferent*): There was something in her that . . . anyhow, I believe it's better that that woman has left.

FLAGMAN: Which one, sir?

MAN: That one, the one who had picked up a white flower . . .

FLAGMAN: I didn't notice that. . . .

MAN: No? (*He looks at the* FLAGMAN *dejectedly.*) But, really, haven't you seen the other one?

FLAGMAN: What other one?

MAN: The one that I'm looking for.

FLAGMAN: I don't know who it can be. . . .

MAN: One who is wearing a white flower, but who isn't the one that you saw a moment ago.

FLAGMAN (*harshly*): I saw the one that you aren't looking for, and the one you're looking for I didn't see!

MAN (*irritated*): Can't you be useful for anything? What the devil are you good for?

(*Loud train whistle.*)

FLAGMAN: What did you say?

MAN (*shouting*): What the devil are you good for!

(*Green light of the semaphore. The* TRAIN *crosses the back of the stage very slowly.*)

FLAGMAN (*in a distant voice*): The trains from the North travel toward the South, the trains from the North travel toward the South, the trains from the North travel toward the South, the trains from the North travel toward the South (*etc.*).

(*The* MAN *covers his head with his hands, desperate. The* FLAGMAN *repeats his refrain while the* TRAIN *passes by slowly. Before it leaves the stage, the curtain falls gently.*)

CURTAIN

❧ Remington 22

Gustavo Andrade Rivera

(Colombia)

Gustavo Andrade Rivera

Gustavo Andrade Rivera was born in 1921 in Neiva, the capital of Huila—one of the smallest and least populated of the Colombian provinces. He spent his first thirty-eight years there, where the majority of his literary efforts appeared in the local newspapers. ■ Though it was home, the insularity and the artistic barrenness of the provincial capital became unbearable. Andrade Rivera had other dreams. If they were to be realized he must leave. In 1959, with very little money in his pockets and no job awaiting him, he left for Bogotá, where he has since resided. ■ In the Colombian capital Andrade Rivera turned to drama for the first time. Though he has written movie scenarios and some short stories, his major contribution to Colombian letters lies in the theater, particularly the one-act play. His more important works include *El hombre que vendía talento* (1959), *Historias para quitar el miedo* (1961), *Remington 22* (1961), *El camino, Hola allá adentro,* and *El hijo del caudillo se quita la camisa* (1963). ■ *Remington 22* differs from the rest of the plays in this collection both in technique and emphasis. Dialogue does not carry all of the action here. Andrade Rivera uses only those words necessary for the audience to understand what is taking place on stage. The action is displayed in a series of pantomimelike tableaux that suggest more poignantly than words the author's anguish at the inhumanity and degradation to which man's blind pride drives him. Though it was directly inspired by the terror that erupted in Colombia at the murder of the liberal leader Jorge Eliecer Gaitán in 1948, *Remington 22* echoes the havoc wreaked anywhere when irresponsible men, bent only upon their hunger for power at any cost, manipulate others to achieve that power.

Remington 22
A Dramatic Piece in Three Tableaux

How can you write about what is happening in Colombia without falling into sectarianism? without producing, above all, a tear-jerker if it is a novel—or a soap opera if it is a question of theater? The answer is puppets!

All that ordinary characters can have of the ridiculous and sectarian disappears—by quintessence, by the exaggeration of the ridiculous and of the sectarian—when puppets are used.

Sectarianism, in the hands of puppets, exaggerated by the puppets, loses its condition as such. It diminishes itself. It reduces itself to a thing of puppets.

Nor does the ridiculous exist for puppets. What would otherwise make one laugh—because it is ridiculous—turns out tremendously tragic, distinctly tragic in the hands of puppets.

For that reason, I have chosen to use puppets here—puppet actors. With the exception of Gringo, who is the foreign eye that looks at us, the foreign eye that wonders at our dangerous puppet game, and of the Mother and the Father, who are the victims, creatures of pure sorrow, all of the characters are puppets.

The first tableau takes place at the beginning of the violence. It is night.

The second, the following day. Eleven in the morning.

The succession of events of the third tableau takes place at different hours of the day or night. What really matters is that everything that is happening is actually taking place at the present time.

Characters

FATHER
MOTHER

GRINGO
PUPPET GUSTAVUS
PUPPET GEORGE
PUPPET ISIDOR
PUPPET PUBLIC EMPLOYEE
PUPPET PHOTOGRAPHER
PUPPET ANNOUNCER
PUPPET BLACK ANGEL
PUPPET WHITE ANGEL
PUPPET BICOLORED ANGEL
PUPPET FULL-DRESS ANGEL
PUPPET BLUE NEWSPAPER BOY
PUPPET RED NEWSPAPER BOY
PUPPET BANDITS, three
PUPPET CYCLISTS, three
PUPPET BLUE NEIGHBORS, several, of both sexes
PUPPET RED NEIGHBORS, several, of both sexes
PUPPET QUEEN
PUPPET PEASANTS, several, children and old people, men and women
   In addition, REAL PUPPETS, that is, of cloth and straw in the shape of peasants and of a child

Setting: Black curtains. Neither walls, nor doors, nor windows. At the center, rear, two black caskets. A blue flag on one. A red flag on the other. A wreath on each casket. On each wreath a black ribbon with very legible white letters, which read respectively *Gustavus* and *George*. Gustavus and George are brothers by the same parents. Lighted wax candles. Perhaps no more illumination is needed. Between the two caskets, two wicker chairs.

(*As the curtain rises,* MOTHER *and* FATHER—*remember that* MOTHER, FATHER, *and* GRINGO *are not puppets, but the only real characters— are sitting on the wicker chairs. One should also bear in mind that the* MOTHER *and* FATHER *are the victims, creatures of pure sorrow.*

The MOTHER *has a rosary and is saying her beads quietly, with scarce-*
ly perceptible movements of her lips. The silence is accentuated by
eight strokes of a bell—it is eight in the evening—and by the tolling
of the death knell that comes from a distant church.
    (*The neighbors begin to arrive.* PUPPET BLUE NEIGHBORS—*dressed*
totally in blue enter from stage right. PUPPET RED NEIGHBORS—*dressed*
entirely in red—enter from the other side. They form themselves
into two groups that look at each other with fear and rancor. They
arrange themselves around the coffins: the BLUE NEIGHBORS *around*
the coffin with the blue flag, the RED NEIGHBORS *around the one with*
the red flag. Great tension is evident. There is a moment of extreme
embarrassment in which it appears that the two groups of puppets,
face to face, are going to come to blows. Afterward, alternately
(*that is a* PUPPET BLUE NEIGHBOR, *a* PUPPET RED NEIGHBOR, *a* PUPPET
BLUE NEIGHBOR, *etc.*), *they approach the parents to express their con-*
dolences. The parents, in the midst of the mummery of the neighbors,
remain aloof, with a sorrow that places them above what is happen-
ing at their side. As they express their condolences, the neighbors
bump into one another, get in each other's way, push one another.
Finally each group leaves the same way it entered. Patent funeral
music is heard. The darkness becomes more pronounced. The flames
of the candles quiver as if about to go out. From the distant church
comes the knell of a bell.)

First Tableau

MOTHER: Eight thirty?

FATHER (*after a silence, neither so long that it empties the room, nor*
so short that it spoils the dramatic effect of the moment. The same
applies to pauses in the conversation that follows): Eight thirty.

MOTHER: Tomorrow . . . the funeral?

FATHER: Yes . . . tomorrow the funeral.

MOTHER: At what time?

FATHER: The priest said at eleven.

MOTHER: Will anything . . . happen?

FATHER: They are wrought up . . . the Blues on account of Gustavus's death . . . the Reds on account of George's death. . . . I'm indeed afraid that something will happen.

MOTHER (*getting up*): My God! More dead, more dead! How did this begin, my God?

FATHER (*also gets up*): How did it begin? (*He pauses.*) How do rivers begin? How does a swollen river that roars and drags you down and everything that is yours, begin? Does a spring of water, its source lost among the folds of a mountain, know of the destruction, of the desolation and death that it's going to cause in the valley? How did it begin? . . . I'd prefer to know how it's going to end. When it's going to end.

MOTHER: It doesn't matter to me how it's going to end . . . because it already ended. For us, everything's over now.

FATHER: I believe that it's beginning. . . .

MOTHER (*angrily*): It already ended, do you hear me?! It ended. There's the end. (*She points at the coffins.*) However, I do want to know (*Calming down*) how all this began. I want to know what sin we committed and when we committed it because this is a punishment! (*Directly to the* FATHER:) Have you committed that sin?

FATHER: The river never returns to its source . . . unless it is in the form of a cloud.

MOTHER: I'm not a river, do you understand me? I'm a mother! And I swear to you by God, by . . . by those two dead sons . . . that I knew how to be a mother, a good mother!

FATHER: And I . . . ?

MOTHER: You also were a good father. . . . My God, how did this begin? (*To the* FATHER:) Tell me! You know because you're a man. . . . because these things are men's things!

FATHER: In what do the Blues distinguish themselves from the Reds?

MOTHER: The Blues are bad! Bad! They go dressed in blue, with blue flags, screaming, shouting insults against the Reds, armed to the teeth, and killing . . . killing until the victim was our son George. (*She hurls herself weeping on George's casket.*)

FATHER: And the Reds?

MOTHER (*now embracing Gustavus's coffin*): They too are bad! Bad! They go dressed in red, with red flags, screaming, shouting insults against the Blues, armed to the teeth and killing . . . killing until the victim was our son Gustavus. (*She weeps over his casket.*)

FATHER: And twenty years ago . . . were you capable of distinguishing a Blue from a Red?

MOTHER (*lifts her head, surprised by the question*): No. . . .

FATHER: Nor I either. It's a difference that I never could understand. . . . Twenty years ago what were my friend Rocco and my friend Isidor?

MOTHER (*still more disconcerted*): Well . . . well, Isidor was the one who carried the nails . . . and Rocco was the one who carried the crown of thorns in the Good Friday processions. Rocco was the one who paid for the High Mass, the fireworks, and the whole celebration of his patron saint, Saint Rocco; and the feast of Saint Isidor, also with a lot of fireworks and High Mass, was paid for by Isidor.

FATHER: Yes. And all their fight about blue and red consisted in which one went to the procession with the more stiffly starched shirt; and in which one used up more fireworks on the feast of his respective patron saint. But years later, Isidor and Rocco shot one another dead in the yard of the church—and took with them fifteen

more from either side—to the shouts of Long Live the Blue Party,
Down with the Red Party, Down with the Blue Bastards.

MOTHER: That doesn't answer my question on how this started.

FATHER: Really, do you want to know how this began?

MOTHER: I want to know.

FATHER: Do you think that that's going to satisfy you?

MOTHER: Even if it doesn't satisfy me.

FATHER: It's going to hurt you.

MOTHER: Now nothing can hurt more deeply.

FATHER: What were our sons?

MOTHER (*answering differently from the* FATHER's *expectation*): They
were good and handsome. Gustavus (*She embraces Gustavus's coffin lovingly. She fondles it as if it were a cradle or Gustavus himself.*) was tall and slender. He had . . . he almost didn't have, do you
remember that he almost didn't have nails on his two little toes? (*She
smiles sweetly.*) George (*She goes to George's coffin and also embraces it.*) was smaller and heavier. Do you remember . . . do you
remember that when he had the measles he left his room, and the
measles dried up and he was covered with spots that almost wouldn't
go away? (*She smiles, almost laughs.*)

FATHER (*allowing himself to be carried away by the memories that
the* MOTHER *evokes*): I hate bathtubs ever since the day that Gustavus fell head first into one, and almost drowned on us.

MOTHER: Yes, yes, and you succeeded in pulling him out. . . . He
didn't swallow a lot of water.

FATHER: What a brute that doctor was who almost let George lose
his arm. He broke it one Saturday . . . one Saturday afternoon, and
that doctor didn't want to operate on him until Monday. And on
Monday his arm was horrible, all swollen and purple.

MOTHER: Thanks to our Lady of Lourdes we saved it. It was gangrene. On Monday he had gangrene, and the water of Lourdes worked the miracle.

FATHER: They grew. . . .

MOTHER: They grew. . . . I liked to go out with them for they took me by the arm and they lead me in this way, along the street. There was always someone who would say to me: "How big your sons are. They are some men." I liked them to tell me that. . . . I liked it. And they liked it too.

FATHER: I liked it when they told me, "Your sons are very intelligent, the best students." Then I would brag a little. "The fact is that that's hereditary," I'd say.

(*A short silence follows.*)

MOTHER: Anthony.

FATHER: What?

MOTHER (*stubbornly*): How did this begin?

FATHER: Do you insist?

MOTHER: I insist. Be good and tell me.

FATHER: I repeat that it's going to hurt.

MOTHER: I repeat that it doesn't matter to me.

FATHER: Who caused Gustavus's death?

MOTHER (*rapidly*): The Reds.

FATHER: And George's?

MOTHER: (*rapidly*): The Blues.

FATHER: And what were Gustavus and George?

MOTHER: Gustavus and George. (*She stops suddenly.*) . . . But are you accusing them? They're dead and you accuse them?

FATHER: I told you that it was going to hurt.

MOTHER: They're dead. My sons are dead and you accuse them! You accuse them because Gustavus was a Blue and George was a Red, isn't that it? Well, the one was Blue and the other was Red, but it isn't bad to be Blue or to be Red except when one's bad from within. My sons, hear it well, my sons (*Emphasis on "my sons" whenever she says it*) never were part of the Blues and of the Reds who kill and murder, of those who killed them. They were good . . . good and brotherly. They loved one another. . . . Their only fights, foolish fights between brothers, were over the typewriter.

FATHER: That's it! The typewriter. What else were they?

MOTHER: I'll tell you, I'll tell you! My sons used to write, and writing isn't bad. They wrote very well. A moment ago you said that they were very intelligent, and they were. They wrote very well.

FATHER: They wrote very well. And to write isn't bad. But what did our sons write? Lies! Blue lies and Red lies for the damned newspapers in the capital! Lies that were blown up there. As if that weren't bad enough, there they enlarged those lies! They were brotherly, yes, but I knew that something bad was beginning when Gustavus said that he was going to write for the Blue newspaper, and George replied that he was a Red and that he would write, also, in the Red newspaper. I knew at that moment that something was beginning that would end badly. Violence begins when brothers are divided.

MOTHER: I don't believe it. I can't believe it!

FATHER: Who wrote this? (*He advances determinedly toward the corner of the stage, which suddenly is lighted, breaking the semi-darkness there until this moment. Only the corner is lighted, and the rest remains in shadow. Other spots on stage and in the orchestra will be lighted in the same way when so indicated. In the corner there is a table with its chair. On the table, an old typewriter. Side by side, on the floor, blue papers and red ones folded like news-*

papers. The FATHER *looks through the heap of red papers. He takes one and advances with it to stage center, leaving the lighted area in the corner. When he begins to read, practically in the dark,* GEORGE *comes out from the rear, sits down at the typewriter and begins to write.* GEORGE *is a puppet dressed in white. He wears a red mask.*) Who, who wrote this? Listen: Today the parish priest of this locality accused the Reds of being the perpetrators of Christ's death and incited the Blues to form armies with which to put an end to the Reds, under the pain of mortal sin. The good Catholics who are Reds withdrew from the church. In the yard they were attacked with stones by the Blue forces prepared beforehand by the priest and the mayor. (*Light on the* FATHER, *while the typewriter is left in darkness.*) I ask you again, who wrote this?

MOTHER (*coming into the light*): It seems to be a dispatch of George's . . . surely to bother the priest a little.

FATHER: Yes, it's a dispatch of George's. But if he only wanted to bother a little, he should have continued bothering with his irreverent remarks about the Immaculate Conception. Because to twist a sermon on the seven last words . . . is not to bother just a little.

(*At the other end of the stage, a pulpit is lighted. At the same time a tape recorder in full view on the pulpit begins to run. The priest's voice is heard—at first hazy, then clearer.*)

PRIEST'S VOICE: Thus, then, my brothers, Jesus died on the cross because of sinners. And the sinners of all times, those of yesterday and those of today—above all, those of today. They keep on killing Jesus. Where are the Catholics, the good Catholics, of courage and of action? If Jesus keeps on dying, it is because of cowardice. We're cowards, incapable of defending Jesus Christ. And we shall condemn ourselves, because heaven is only for the brave. We shall condemn ourselves because the weak will never be able to be part of the Blue Army of Paradise.

(*The lights darken on the pulpit and focus on the* PUPPET RED NEWSPAPER BOY *who is in the audience, with a lot of red newspapers.*)

PUPPET RED NEWSPAPER BOY: Extra! Extra! Extra! The Red newspaper with news of the outrages of the Blues against the Reds. The Red National Board of Directors complains to the bishop of the parish priest's outrages. Extra! Extra! Extra! From the church they're shooting against the Reds who were leaving mass peacefully. Extra! Extra! Extra!

(PUPPET RED NEWSPAPER BOY *ends by going up on the stage and leaving. Light on the* FATHER.)

FATHER (*pointing at the audience*): Look at the faces of the people. Blue and Red alike. They're surprised, stunned because everything is a lie. Days later, it was the feast of St. Isidor. My old friend Isidor, as he does every year, went to burn his fireworks and his innocuous skyrockets in the churchyard.

(*Lights on yard of the church, where the pulpit was before. There can be a curtain, some scenery, or simply an imaginary churchyard.* PUPPET ISIDOR *and two or three more puppets are there. They perform the small-town pantomime of setting off fireworks, accompanied by the corresponding sound effects. After setting off a few,* PUPPET ISIDOR *begins to dedicate them.*)

PUPPET ISIDOR: This one's in honor of my patron, St. Isidor. (*He sets it off.*) This one's in honor of the most Holy Virgin. (*He sets it off.*) This one's in honor of St. Joseph. (*He sets it off.*) This one's for the priest.

ACCOMPANYING PUPPET: Don't be stupid, Isidor, for you're throwing them toward the church and they're going to go off inside there.

(*As a matter of fact—loudest sound effect—the skyrocket explodes inside the church. There is panic, shouts, and the running of people —*PUPPETS—*who were in the church. After a few moments of tumult, lights on the* FATHER *who pokes among the blue newspapers. With a newspaper in his hand, he goes toward stage center, moving out of the light, while* GUSTAVUS *comes into the light, that is, to the type-*

writer, where he begins to type. GUSTAVUS—PUPPET GUSTAVUS—*is the same as* PUPPET GEORGE. *He is* GUSTAVUS *now because he wears a blue mask.*)

FATHER (*in the darkness, while* GUSTAVUS *writes*): Gustavus wrote this wild statement: The Reds, in an act of barbarism, fired on the priest and the Catholics who were attending High Mass last Sunday. Fortunately the Blues reacted courageously and punished the miserable aggressors, but there are several wounded, some seriously. The victims of the Red massacre are being taken care of by doctors who arrived from the capital since the Red doctor of the locality refused to attend them.

PUPPET BLUE NEWSPAPER BOY (*light on him, in the audience*): Extra! Extra! Extra! The Blue newspaper with the news of the Red assault of a church. Extra! Extra! Extra! Priest and Catholics shot by Red rabble commanded by the hospital doctor. Extra! Extra! Extra! Violence breaks loose. Twenty-five Blues dead. Orphans and widows cry out for justice. (*The* PUPPET BLUE NEWSPAPER BOY *goes up onto the stage and leaves.*)

MOTHER (*light on her and on the* FATHER *at the center*): Gustavus was playful. He liked to tease George. And that business about the doctor must have been to get even on account of his being forbidden to visit the doctor's daughter.

FATHER: He could be funny in another way. At the expense of Don Fidel's breeding mules . . . or Don Clement's celibate grandparents. He could keep on inventing reigns until all of the girls were queens of something. Look! Look at those faces! (*Pointing at the audience:*) There's no longer surprise or wonder. Already fear and rancor begin. Hate! From then on, the news, as exaggerated and full of mistakes as it was, had a basis of truth. . . . No one knows how much brush can be set on fire with a single match.

PUPPET BLUE NEWSPAPER BOY (*in the audience*): Extra! Extra! Extra! Blue paperr . . .

PUPPET RED NEWSPAPER BOY (*also in the audience*): Extra! Extra! Extra! Red paperr . . .

PUPPET BLUE NEWSPAPER BOY (*in another place in the orchestra, closer to the stage*): Extra! Extra! Extra! Blue paperr . . .

PUPPET RED NEWSPAPER BOY (*also closer to the stage*): Extra! Extra! Extra! Red paperr . . .

PUPPET BLUE NEWSPAPER BOY (*on the stage*): Extra! Extra! Extra! Blue paperr . . . (*He goes off to one side.*)

PUPPET RED NEWSPAPER BOY (*from the stage, after which he leaves*): Extra! Extra! Extra! Red paperr . . .

(*Simultaneously with the shouts of the* PUPPET NEWSPAPER BOYS, GUS-TAVUS *and* GEORGE *appear—illuminated—in the corner with the type-writer. However since* GUSTAVUS *and* GEORGE *are the same actor, with a different mask, the role reduces itself to a change of mask: blue mask when the* PUPPET BLUE NEWSPAPER BOY *shouts, red mask when the* PUPPET RED NEWSPAPER BOY *shouts. The change is made in view of the audience, with the mask which is not used on the table beside the machine. With the exit of the* NEWSPAPER BOYS, GUSTAVUS *and* GEORGE *remain in the dark.*)

FATHER (*at stage center, with the* MOTHER, *both beneath the light*): The rest is there. (*He points to the mountains of blue and red news-papers, which at that moment are lighted.*) And there . . . . (*He points to the two coffins.*) And there . . . and there . . . and there . . . . (*He points toward different sides of the stage.*) Wherever there is a burned ranch, a lost harvest . . . , a cross at the edge of the road. Now they kill one another for their pair of colors. For their damned blue. For their damned red. But this is only the beginning. Later they'll kill . . . for nothing, for the sake of killing, simply for the pleasure of killing. That's why I said that it's not important to know how this began, but how it's going to end, when it's going to end.

MOTHER: How can those who are now victims be guilty?

FATHER: The river never returns to its source.

MOTHER: They killed them on me! Blue murderers who killed my son George! Red murderers who killed my son Gustavus. Damn them! It was with a gun! It was with a gun! (*She leaves.*)

FATHER: Where are you going?

MOTHER: I'll be right back. (*She returns at once with a gun.*) We're going to throw this away. We're going to burn it, to destroy it, because this is to blame for what's happening to us . . . to us . . . to this town.

(*She throws the gun to* FATHER *who stretches his hands to catch it and puts it in the light so that it is seen that it is a 22-caliber Remington.*)

FATHER: Do you really believe that this is to blame?

MOTHER: Didn't they die by the gun? (*She points toward the sons.*) Aren't you saying that this is scarcely beginning? Won't it be a gun that tomorrow brings death again? Isn't what you have in your hands a gun?

FATHER: Yes, it's a 22-caliber Remington.

MOTHER: Then, destroy it, if you don't want it to destroy us!

FATHER: This gun is a poor useless gun, always waiting for some thieves who never came. I don't deny that the gun, the gun of others, commits the violence. Bullets from a Red gun put an end to Gustavus. For George, it was bullets from a Blue gun. If tomorrow there are more dead, it will be by bullets of both colors. But . . . who armed the people? (*Slapping the newspapers*:) Will I need to read you more of these papers? I know something more powerful, more dangerous than guns.

MOTHER: What can be more dangerous than a gun in the hands of the murderers of my sons?

FATHER: This! (*He throws the gun on the table and takes up the typewriter.*) This, in the hands of the two fools of our sons.

MOTHER: No! No! (*She draws near and feels it lovingly.*) Our sons' old typewriter. How can you think such a thing?

FATHER: It's a Remington.

MOTHER: A Remington?

FATHER: Model 1922.

MOTHER: My God! A Remington 22! (*She turns in anguish toward the two coffins.*)

CURTAIN

Second Tableau

Setting: Bicolored street, blue on one side—the audience's right— and red on the other. No details. Two completely plain panels, painted red and blue. At the most, patches, big brush strokes in white or black, to suggest buildings.

(*When the curtain rises, the neighbors appear carrying and surrounding the coffins of Gustavus and George.* PUPPET BLUE NEIGHBORS—*only men—carry the coffin with the blue flag.* PUPPET RED NEIGHBORS—*men—the one with the red flag. All carry guns. In the center—obviously unarmed—*MOTHER *and* FATHER. *It is a march toward the cemetery that, perhaps, could begin from the orchestra. When the procession arrives at stage rear, it is lost from view. There is a brief darkening. Now the neighbors return without the parents. They stop at the edge of the stage, because at that moment, coming from the rear, along the sidewalk of corresponding color, appear* PUPPET BLUE NEWSPAPER BOY *and* PUPPET RED NEWSPAPER BOY *hawking their merchandise.*)

PUPPET BLUE NEWSPAPER BOY: Extra! Extra! Extra!

PUPPET RED NEWSPAPER BOY: Extra! Extra! Extra!

PUPPET BLUE NEWSPAPER BOY: Murdered by the Reds, correspondent for this newspaper! Extra! Extra! Extra!

PUPPET RED NEWSPAPER BOY: Murdered by the Blues, correspondent for this newspaper! Extra! Extra! Extra!

(*This course of events is the spark that was wanting. The* REDS *and the* BLUES *buy their respective newspapers. As the* NEWSPA-PER BOYS *leave, they read the news. They become incensed. They threaten one another from group to group—all in pantomime—and they end by attacking one another. The site of the encounter is in the middle of the street. Darkness, shouts, and shots. Afterward absolute silence. A gentle light shows a scrambled heap of dead* NEIGHBORS, *fallen guns, and scattered newspapers. The* NEWSPAPER BOYS *appear, along the respective sidewalks, walking toward stage rear. They do not shout. They go slowly, with a total indifference for the dead. After them come darkness and a wind that ruffles the papers over the fallen. From the distant church come the twelve strokes of the noon bell and the knells of the angelus.*)

CURTAIN

Third Tableau

(*The stage is empty and in complete darkness. The voices and the noises that follow can be recorded.*)

VOICE OF CHIEF BANDIT: You, what are you?

VOICE OF A FRIGHTENED ONE: I . . . am probably a Blue.

VOICE OF CHIEF BANDIT: He says that he's a Blue, boys.

(*Close firing of a gun. And the thud of a body falling.*)

VOICE OF CHIEF BANDIT: And you . . . ? What are you?

HOPEFUL VOICE: Red. I'm a Red.

VOICE OF CHIEF BANDIT: This one's a Red, boys.

(*Firing of gun and thud.*)

VOICE OF CHIEF BANDIT: Let's see . . . you! What the devil are you?

VOICE WITHOUT ANY HOPE: Nothing, nothing. My God, I'm . . . I'm a farmer. I did nothing.

VOICE OF CHIEF BANDIT: Aha . . . so you want to save yourself. (*Guffaw of the* CHIEF *and guffaw of the other* BANDITS.) So nothing. (*General guffaws.*) So a farmer. And are you thinking that the others were learned men? (*More laughs.*) Well, it's better for you to be a farmer because that way you'll die with your pants on. That's the difference between the educated and the farmers: that farmers die with their pants on because they sleep with their pants on. And if it turns out that you're one of the educated ones—a doctor or something underneath those pants stinking of piss—it won't be the first one that we've shot, damn it! Lots of doctors in shorts appear from under their beds when we attack a town. (*Laughs.*) Surprised petty doctors, frightened, cowards, that allow their wives and daughters to be used, without opening their mugs not even to let loose a "damn." And they allow themselves to be killed kneeling, asking for pardon, with their revolvers underneath their pillows. Do you know what you are? Well, a wise guy, that's what you are. Only you're too smart, and that's bad with us. With us no one is too smart, except to drop dead. (*Again laughs.*) Well, you're going to see . . . wise guy! You're going to see right now! Fire, boys!

(*Third discharge. Third body that falls. Noise of armed persons who leave. And then, in the midst of the most absolute silence, it begins to grow light. The rear part of the stage is a stark white curtain—a kind of screen which, as lights are played on it, projects, enlarges, and even deforms the shadows of the actions. In back of this curtain is the scenery proper—a nocturnal and sad peasant atmosphere. It may be another white curtain on which one has drawn in black.*)

(*To the left of the audience, what was once a peasant ranch, now destroyed by fire, still smoking, is seen. On the other side—right—is the* GRINGO. *His back to the audience, he types on an old Remington. His desk is a big rickety box or a board that rests on two piles of bricks.* GRINGO *is a foreign correspondent. The names of the presses that he represents are written on very visible slats nailed to poles, like the traffic signs at crossroads.*

(*In the center, the three murdered farmers. They are three real puppets. The straw that fills them should come out from their extremities in the manner of hands and feet. The head is a coconut on which are roughly drawn the eyes, nose, and mouth. They are thrown ridiculously like three fallen scarecrows. Their shadows are projected, enlarged, and deformed on the curtain in the rear.*

(*The* GRINGO, *engrossed in his work, does not look to either side. It is obvious that he is writing about what has just happened. Only the click of the Remington is heard.*

(PUPPET BLACK ANGEL *enters. He is an angel, but he is a puppet. Remember that all of the characters—except the* MOTHER, FATHER, *and* GRINGO—*are puppets that must speak and act and behave as such. Of course, he has wings. He looks surprised at the puppets on the floor, at the* GRINGO, *at the audience, everywhere. He does not understand what has happened. He respects the glances. He approaches the puppets; he raises their arms and lets them fall. They fall heavily, lifelessly. He looks at the* GRINGO. *He motions to him and ends by calling him at the same time that he points at the puppets.*)

PUPPET BLACK ANGEL (*with the voice of a puppet, but soft and sweet because he is a puppet angel*): Gringo . . . Gringo . . . (*The* GRINGO *continues typing, without paying attention.* PUPPET BLACK ANGEL *calls again in a louder voice:*) Gringo, Gringo! (*The* GRINGO *still does not pay attention. He types vigorously. For the third time the* PUPPET BLACK ANGEL *points at the fallen puppets and calls:*) Gringo! Gringo!

GRINGO (*almost without turning*): Okay . . . okay. . . .

(*The* GRINGO *has stretched his left arm and moves his hand affirmatively. With that he insinuates that he is informed. He starts to write again.* PUPPET BLACK ANGEL, *with a certain dignity, with a certain unction in his gesture, bends over the fallen puppets and picks them up: two in his right hand and one in his left. He leaves with them. The light goes out slowly. The last thing that is seen is the* GRINGO, *beating the Remington, that is, the* GRINGO's *back. Then, surprisingly, the cries of a woman are heard from the back of the theater—Help, Help, Help! From the orchestra aisle* PUPPET FARM WOMAN *runs, pursued by the three* PUPPET BANDITS. *While they advance toward the stage, it is lighted again.*

(*The same set as before: the smoking ranch, the* GRINGO *typing. Again, the murdered peasants, that is, the puppets on the floor in the same posture.* PUPPET FARM WOMAN *and* PUPPET BANDITS, *pursued and pursuers—she with her cries of Help!—go up on to the stage which they cross and recross, jumping over the puppets on the floor. There are moments in which the* PUPPET BANDITS *manage to seize her arm, or her skirt, but she breaks loose and the pursuit continues. Finally, they run behind the white curtain in the rear, and it is then that* PUPPET FARM WOMAN *is finally overtaken and conquered. The shadows projected on the curtain show when she falls giving a most powerful cry—Heellp!—and the* PUPPET BANDITS *in a confused heap, pushing each other, each one seeking to be the first. Gradual darkness. The last thing that is seen is the* GRINGO's *back.*

(*When the light returns, moments later,* PUPPET WHITE ANGEL *sits up in the place where* PUPPET FARM WOMAN *fell. He is white because he is dressed in white, as opposed to the black one who is dressed in black. On sitting up, he remains a moment with his arms stretched and his hands, open because they are holding something, on the floor. When he stands, it is seen that what he has in his hands is a puppet child—a real puppet, of rag and straw. He shows it to the* GRINGO *who says, "Okay, Okay," and continues writing with his back to the audience.* PUPPPET WHITE ANGEL, *somewhat confused, somewhat disoriented, starts to leave. He becomes aware, then, of the puppets on the floor. His confusion increases. He does not know what to do. Finally, his dignity and his angel's composure lost, he picks it all up helter-skelter, and leaves. Brief blackout.*

(*On the stage, lighted again, now appear the offices of the governor, the mayor's office, the Section of Justice, and the Rehabilitation
Center. They are barely doors with their corresponding signs. Each
door is only a simple wood frame. The background continues to be
the white curtain, lighted in order that scenery that is behind shows
through, suggesting abstract silhouettes of buildings which can be
another curtain with sketches in black.* GRINGO *is at stage center, almost at the edge of the stage, his back turned, writing.*

(PUPPET PEASANTS *of all ages, men and women, enter. They come
laden with their peasant belongings, from the useful things to the
useless and improbable; all those things which one grasps hurriedly,
when flight is imperative. Thus is started a pilgrimage—a sorrowful
pilgrimage of puppets—from door to door, from office to office.*

(*They go first to the governor's office. Semblance of knocking at
the door. The* PUPPET PUBLIC EMPLOYEE *comes out. There is dialogue
among the puppets, without words, only with gestures. It is evident
that the* PUPPET PEASANTS *are exiles in search of justice, of help. They
want to speak with the governor because they think that he can help
them.* PUPPET PUBLIC EMPLOYEE *tells them that the governor regrets
deeply the tragedy of the exiles. He wants to help them and he is
going to help them, but now he is too busy to take care of them. The
governor recommends that they speak with the mayor.* PUPPET PUBLIC
EMPLOYEE, *very zealous, points toward the mayor's office. The* PUPPET
PEASANTS *resign themselves. It is necessary to go to the mayor's office.
They are already in motion. At that moment the* PUPPET PHOTOGRA-
PHER *comes out and makes them go back. Pose, flash. Now, yes, to
the mayor's office. In the mayor's office the scene is repeated: dialogue, photograph, and the suggestion to go to the Section of Justice
because the mayor is very busy.* PUPPET PUBLIC EMPLOYEE *and* PUPPET
PHOTOGRAPHER *of the mayor's office are the same ones as were in the
governor's office. They simply go from one office to another in full
view of the audience. From the Section of Justice—there is no puppet photographer here, but always the same gesticulated dialogues,
always the same* PUPPET PUBLIC EMPLOYEE—*they are sent to the Rehabilitation Center.*

(From the Rehabilitation Center back to the governor's office.
The PUPPET PEASANT pantomime says no, that they were already there,
that they do not want more repetitions, more deceptions. And resigned, tired, overcome, they start stretching out. They start piling
on the floor, while the PUPPET PUBLIC EMPLOYEE and the PUPPET PHOTOG-
RAPHER take the placards off the four doors. The night's shadows
prolong the tragic shadows of the peasants, their accumulation, their
misery, on the lighted white curtain at the back. Like a new joke, the
three PUPPET CYCLISTS and the PUPPET ANNOUNCER cross along the back
of the curtain. Of course, no bicycles. The CYCLISTS peddle vigorously, preceded by the SPORTS ANNOUNCER—panting, gesticulating, mi-
crophone in hand—but all in pantomime, this time one that is almost
a ballet. After them—his pantomime like that of the solitary cyclists
who have fallen behind—PUPPET BICOLORED ANGEL appears. He is
white from the waist up and wears black sport shorts, his hairy legs
in view. The PUPPET QUEENS follow.

(The QUEENS are the following: QUEEN OF THE NEW WAVE, QUEEN OF
THE WEEK WITHOUT STRIKES, QUEEN OF TOURISM WITHOUT SMUGGLING,
QUEEN OF THE ABSENTEE LEGISLATORS, QUEEN OF THE FLIGHTS OF THE PRIS-
ONERS, QUEEN OF THE SPECIAL INVESTIGATORS, QUEEN OF THE SALE OF THE
NATIONAL RAILROAD, QUEEN OF THE COLD PEACE. Of course, they are
puppets—PUPPET QUEENS. QUEEN OF THE NEW WAVE is a botch, a hodge-
podge of the latest "isms" of all those little women, who promenade
their physical dishevelments and their spiritual no's through the
world. QUEEN OF THE ABSENTEE LEGISLATORS is announced but does not
appear. She is absent. QUEEN OF THE COLD PEACE is a cruel joke in view
of what is happening everywhere, especially on the stage.

(And so on, with great imagination, with great inventiveness, the
director of the play must achieve with each queen the particular
caricature of the reign she represents as well as the general caricature of our stupid passion for royalty. The seven queens are one
single person, one actress capable of giving, in seconds—with the
right direction—the physical and spiritual changes that each reign
needs. Otherwise resort to seven women. In any case the PUPPET
QUEENS appear and disappear in the frames that formerly served as

offices. With the stage in darkness, a frame is lighted and a QUEEN
appears. Said frame is darkened. Another is lighted and a different
QUEEN *appears. And so on until all the* QUEENS *are presented. It is a*
play of lights and of QUEENS, *rapid, lively. The* QUEEN *appears in the*
lighted frame by jumping from the darkness in the back. She greets
the public and executes the pantomime that suits her characteriza-
tion. A second after each QUEEN, PUPPET FULL-DRESS ANGEL *leaps into*
the light, in front of the frame. He is an angel because he is wearing
tails. He is in charge of introducing the QUEENS.)

PUPPET FULL-DRESS ANGEL (*announcing after he bows*): Ladies and
Gentlemen, . . . the Queen of . . . the New Wave . . . ! (*In like manner,*
jumping from frame to frame, he presents them. The only one not
there is the QUEEN OF THE ABSENTEE LEGISLATORS. *At this point:*) Ladies
and Gentlemen, . . . the Queen of . . . the Absentee Legislators . . . !
(*He notices that there is no queen, he makes some puppet gesture*
in accord with the situation, and explains:) Ladies and Gentlemen,
. . . the Queen of the Absentee Legislators . . . is in session.

(*Up to this point, everything is normal. The play of lights and of the*
QUEENS *has been rapid, quick, but normal. From here on the rhythm*
accelerates. New introductions of the QUEENS *follow—all the intro-*
ductions necessary—with a speed that increases until a dazzling,
unreal, nightmarish atmosphere is created. The frames light up and
go out and the QUEENS *appear and disappear with such speed that*
PUPPET FULL-DRESS ANGEL *loses the synchronism. He arrives late to an-*
nounce them. He brakes, skids, comes back, tries to shout their
names. He seems a madman. Finally, he begins to mix up the names:
Queen of the Legislator Smugglers, Queen of the Prisoner Tourists,
Queen of the Investigators of the New Wave, Queen of the Tourism
Without Legislators, Queen of the Week Without the National Rail-
road, Queen of the Peace of the Strike, etc., playing verbal games
with the names of the reigns. Finally he stops, with his hands on his
head, and he shouts:)

PUPPET FULL-DRESS ANGEL: Queens! Queens! Queens! (*Until the*
shouting softens to a sob:) queens . . . queens . . . queens . . . (*The*

curtain falls. And the sobs of the PUPPET FULL-DRESS ANGEL *are still heard*:) queens . . . queens . . . queens.

(When the curtain falls, GRINGO—*who has not stopped typing for a single moment—remains outside, in the view of the audience. With all calm, he gathers up his paper, his machine, his signs. He comes down from the stage and leaves by the orchestra aisle. He stops for a moment in order to ask one of the spectators in the first row a question.)*

GRINGO: Where is the post office, please? I've a very interesting story about this country, to be published in my newspapers, and I have to send it immediately. *(On realizing that the spectator does not understand him, he repeats the question in Spanish, with a strong foreign accent.)* ¿Por favor, dónde queda el correo? Tengo una historia muy interestante sobre este país y debo mandarla inmediatamente a mis periódicos. *(He pretends he has received an answer and adds, with an indication of his arm:)* That way? Thanks. *(At that moment he stumbles and lets the typewriter fall. Then he exclaims:)* Oh, damn it! *(He picks it up.)* My typewriter. I like it a lot because I bought it very cheaply from a couple that wanted to throw it away. It's very good in spite of its age. Nothing less than a 1922 Remington. A Remington 22. *(He walks toward the exit and leaves.)*

CURTAIN

✎ The Guillotine

Matías Montes Huidobro

(Cuba)

Matías Montes Huidobro

Matías Montes Huidobro was born in Sagua la Grande, a small town in the central province of Las Villas, Cuba, in 1931. Only at considerable personal sacrifice did he finish his university studies, earning a degree in Education from the University of Havana. For several years he worked as a high school teacher. Between 1959 and 1961 he served as a theater critic for the newspaper *Revolución* and for CMBF Television in Havana. ■ *Las cuatro brujas*, awarded honorable mention in 1950 in the National Dramatic Contest sponsored by the theater group Prometeo, marked his debut as a playwright. The following year Montes Huidobro took First Prize in the same contest with his *Sobre las mismas rocas*. In 1959 he wrote an impressive one-act play, *Los acosados*, which not only enjoyed a long run on the stage, but was also published the same year in *Lunes de Revolución*—then the leading organ of young literary talent. ■ In the years immediately preceding his exile in 1961, Montes Huidobro wrote extensively. These works include *La botija* (1960), *Las vacas* (1960), which won first prize in a national contest, and *El tiro por la culata* (1961). Two one-act plays, *Las caretas* and *La puerta perdida*, and a full-length one, *El verano está cerca*, to our knowledge, remain unpublished and unperformed to date. *Gas en los poros* and *La sal de los muertos*, both written in 1961, share with *Los acosados* in a penetrating view, so lucid that it seems a sort of madness, of a reality whose abject, incomprehensible events and values generate a sense of oppression and uselessness. ■ *Guillotine* (*La madre y la guillotina*), written in 1961, discloses, by an elaborate play-within-play technique, the contradictory passions usually unchained at the outset of a revolution. The hatred, the shameless hypocrisy, and the morbid egotism of the daughters—both guilty and therefore doomed— form a sharp contrast to the suffering of the mother, symbol of the Mater Dolorosa, eternally mourning for the victims of that insanity that makes man the indifferent executioner of his fellow. ■ Montes Huidobro is also a writer of fiction as well as a poet. *La anunciación*, a collection of short stories, appeared in 1967. He recently completed a novel and a new play, *Funeral en Teruel*. At present he resides in Honolulu where he is an associate professor of Spanish at the University of Hawaii.

The Guillotine

Characters

MOTHER
ILEANA
SILVIA
HAIRDRESSER

Time and Place: 1959 in Cuba

Setting: The back of the stage will be dominated by a large, over-whelmingly impressive mural, on which a guillotine appears. Stage front, two folding chairs. On a slightly elevated platform, two other folding chairs and a small table. The front of the stage, where the two chairs are, is lighted.

(*The* MOTHER, *crestfallen and worried, is seated.* ILEANA *stands, facing the audience. She then turns toward the* MOTHER.)

ILEANA: What part do you have in this play?

MOTHER (*always worried*): I'm the mother.

ILEANA: Whose mother?

MOTHER: Yours and the manicurist's.

ILEANA: Of the two of us?

MOTHER: Yes, of the two of you.

ILEANA: I suppose it must be a difficult part.

MOTHER: Not really; it's the same character all along.

ILEANA: A bit complicated, huh? The same thing happens to me. Authors always complicate things. In real life everything's simpler.

MOTHER (*distressed*): Are you sure?

95

ILEANA (*with disdain*): At least, I'd like to think so.

MOTHER: Do you like the theater?

ILEANA: It's a living.

MOTHER (*seriously*): But do you take it seriously?

ILEANA: Life's a dangerous game in which one must defend herself like a tiger.

MOTHER: I don't understand you very well.

ILEANA: Why?

MOTHER: Ileana . . . your name is Ileana, isn't it?

ILEANA: Yes.

MOTHER: Don't you think that we ought to get to know each other little by little? After all, we're so close. . . .

ILEANA (*with a certain ill-mannered indifference*): As you like . . .

MOTHER: I wouldn't want to become fond of you. But perhaps it's inevitable. I'm afraid of being disappointed, and that this won't be a play. Have you read the play?

ILEANA: No, but what are you talking about? Aren't they paying you for this?

MOTHER: I'm your mother. I'm afraid that something will happen to you.

ILEANA (*transition. Acting as if she really were the daughter*): Mama, I'll know how to defend myself. Up to now, I've managed well, haven't I?

MOTHER: I can't avoid it, daughter. I'm not at peace. Too many things are happening. Perhaps everything will go wrong for us now.

ILEANA: Bah, the important thing here is not to die. I've always known how to swim so as not to drown. Don't get ahead of things, mama.

MOTHER (*transition. In a more impersonal tone*): I hope to get along well with you. The manicurist has a difficult character.

ILEANA: So I've heard. I detest her, really. I suppose that your being my mother, she'll be my sister. Is she really?

MOTHER (*perplexed, not knowing what to say*): No, I don't think so. . . . But don't be frightened. . . . Actually, I'm not sure of anything . . .

ILEANA: And do you know anything about me?

MOTHER (*hesitantly*): I think. . . . But you'll take offense if I tell you it . . .

ILEANA: No. . . . Speak . . . speak . . .

MOTHER: You . . . you're . . . the mistress . . . of Commander Camacho.

ILEANA: The murderer?

MOTHER (*in a low voice*): Yes. . . . Him . . .

ILEANA: No, but that can't be.

MOTHER: Calm down. . . . Don't get excited . . .

ILEANA (*violently*): And her?

MOTHER (*afraid*): Her?

ILEANA: Yes, the manicurist! Speak!

MOTHER: I don't remember too well. . . . But they speak of a certain Caesar . . . of the Ministry of Education . . . or the Treasury . . . I'm not sure.

ILEANA: Well, you gave me back my peace of mind . . . at least in part. Because if they attribute that business about Commander

Camacho to me and to her the one about that certain Caesar, that
means . . . well, she'll have to keep her mouth shut. . . .

MOTHER: If it were only that way! And nevertheless . . . the fact is
that she has a . . . such a temper . . .

ILEANA: I can't stand her. . . . They've already told me that she
speaks ill of me. . . . And you must know something else. . . . What
do you know?

MOTHER (*evasively*): I can't say. Don't involve me.

ILEANA (*saccharine sweetly*): Of necessity, you must know it,
mama. . . .

MOTHER (*evasively*): It's better not to talk about the matter.

ILEANA: It's about me, mama. Don't you realize it? I'm terrified,
mama. And now that the executions are increasing. . .

MOTHER: Daughter. . .

ILEANA: In these times all of us are in danger. . . . The dictatorship
has fallen. The revolution triumphs. . . . And the revolution is white
and red, immaculate and bloody, isn't it?

MOTHER: My daughter, I know nothing of politics.

ILEANA: And everyone wants to profit from it also. . . . It's a disgusting thing. . . . The idle gossip of the manicurist can go far. You
must know that they're trying to involve me because I slept with
him. . . . As if that were a sin! I had to survive, isn't that true? And
Camacho was good to me, in some ways. I'm not going to deny it.
But there's been nothing else. You know it well. I've never harmed
anyone. But there are people who delight in bearing false witness.

MOTHER: I'm afraid. I find myself in a difficult situation.

ILEANA: Aren't you on my side?

MOTHER (*imploringly*): How could I not be? (*Desperately.*) But she's

my daughter also, don't you realize it? I can't speak of her with you.
I could harm her.

ILEANA (*violently*): But you don't hesitate to harm me. Now yes,
now everyone turns his back on me because I'm down. . . . But when
I was on top. . . . Even my mother, of course. . . . You side with the
other one . . . who feels safe, I don't know why. . . . Because she's
stupid . . . that must be why. . . . Because there's nothing safe here,
nothing that can't fall. . . . As if she didn't have any sins, that snake
in the grass. . . .

MOTHER: Quiet, daughter, quiet.

ILEANA: Would you be so cowardly? Would you allow them to take
me as far as the scaffold without saying a word?

MOTHER: Why the scaffold? What reason would there be, my daughter? You've done nothing. Don't frighten me so.

ILEANA: The slanders, the lies. It never rains but it pours.

MOTHER: No, your death, no, Ileana. I couldn't bear it.

ILEANA: Will you let me know? Will you advise me of the least
danger?

MOTHER: I'll do it . . . I swear it. . . .

(SILVIA, *the manicurist, enters along the platform with the two chairs
and the small table. She brings a tray with nail polish, scissors,
etc. She places it on the small table. This corner of the stage is
illuminated.*)

SILVIA: Good afternoon, have I arrived late for the rehearsal?

ILEANA: Who are you?

SILVIA: I'm the manicurist. (*Drawing nearer, looking at* ILEANA *from
head to toe:*) And you, you're Ileana, no doubt.

ILEANA: Yes.

SILVIA (*disagreeably*): Do you like your part?

ILEANA (*falsely*): It delights me. It's a marvelous character. I'm very happy. And it's the most important part in the comedy.

SILVIA: I understand that it's a drama.

ILEANA: What do you know? The program says that it's a comedy.

SILVIA: Your part, I'd say, isn't too nice.

ILEANA: I've signed a contract. Are you one of those who work just for the love of it?

SILVIA: It's far better than to work just for money, don't you think? For money we're capable of anything. Even of interpreting those parts.

ILEANA: What are you trying to insinuate?

SILVIA: I couldn't take that kind of a part. . . . . It's like a lawyer defending a murderer.

ILEANA: You're very strict with the rest of us.

MOTHER: Ileana, Silvia, girls, please, don't continue along that track. It leads nowhere.

SILVIA: I'm very strict with everything. I can't stand any kind of dirt.

ILEANA: I've read the script. It's better for you not to start washing dirty linen in public. You aren't very clean yourself, shall we say?

SILVIA (*with surprise*): Are you referring to me?

ILEANA: You're asking for it. People who are too perfect bother me. Much worse, those who pretend to be.

SILVIA: I didn't collaborate, directly, with the government.

ILEANA: Now, of course, no one has collaborated. Besides, I've already told you that you're picking on me. And if it's a question of picking on someone and telling them off, I too know how to do it. Being what you are, you ought to go hide in shame.

SILVIA: Camacho . . .

ILEANA: Caesar. . . . Do you hear me, Caesar? . . .

SILVIA: Caesar?

ILEANA: No, don't pretend you don't know.

SILVIA: An acquaintance, perhaps?

ILEANA: An acquaintance who built you a house . . .

SILVIA (addressing the MOTHER): Mama, why are people that way, so mean, so ill-inclined? What wouldn't a mother do for her daughter, and a daughter for her mother? Because that little house was for you, mama, so that you could have a home in your old age. The love and sacrifice of a daughter . . .

ILEANA (crying out): What nerve; my God, what nerve!

SILVIA (turning to ILEANA): Of course, for a woman like you that doesn't matter. The love and sacrifice of a daughter are only words for you. Because that house isn't mine, but mother's . . .

ILEANA: A dirty trick to cover things up in order to . . .

SILVIA: Sour grapes.

ILEANA: And Caesar? What are you going to say when you're asked about him?

SILVIA: Caesar?

ILEANA (imitating her, scoffingly): Caesar? Caesar? And do you think everyone will swallow that?

SILVIA (naturally): What Caesar? Caesar who?

ILEANA: Have you ever seen such nerve?

SILVIA (*without appearing upset, speaking to herself and in a way to the audience*): It'll be necessary to alter this dialogue a little. There are people who don't understand, like this woman, misled and tormented by her conscience. And the worst thing that can happen is that the audience won't understand unless this mix-up is cleared up. She wants to implicate me for no reason at all, and I won't be able to get out of it. People allow themselves to be misled so easily! I'll have to clear up this mix-up over who I really am. Caesar? But which Caesar? Brutus? Caesar? Cleopatra? Elizabeth Taylor? That's nothing more than theater, fantasy. (*Grandiloquently, partly to* ILEANA, *but partly to the audience:*) Look, ignore her. I am who I am. In real life I am a woman who loves the revolution and hates crime. Everyone hates crime, but not as I do! Therefore, I'm in disagreement with certain things—nothing more—about my role and I'm not going to accept them as she does, because she, by God, she doesn't have a reasonable explanation for her behavior. Because she . . .

ILEANA (*throwing herself at* SILVIA): You're lying, you're lying!

SILVIA (*scandalized*): Don't touch me! Don't interrupt me! (*At the top of her voice:*) Because in real life, I'm different and I don't want the audience to boo me and to shout "Informer" whenever I come out on the stage . . .

(*She leaves indignantly, abruptly, arranging her clothes.* ILEANA *is stretched out on the floor. The area of the platform is darkened.*)

ILEANA (*to the* MOTHER): Didn't you hear her? She hates me. She detests me. She's my greatest enemy.

MOTHER: You must calm down. Don't despair. Everything will soon change.

ILEANA: She wants to destroy me. She'll speak with the director in order to harm me. And I have no doubt that she'll do it in my private life too. You already know it. This revolution has reached everywhere, and the opportunists and the hypocrites are mixed up in it too, camouflaged so that no one recognizes them in the underbrush. But I have my plans. I'm not going to let them cut off my head.

MOTHER: Ileana dear, please, this isn't the moment to make enemies. We've enough with what has happened to him.

ILEANA: To him? To him! I've enough trouble on account of him. Now everyone points a finger at me as Camacho's mistress. For all that he's given me! I always wanted a banker, an old banker with loads of money, but I have had very bad luck. Oh, well, why think of that now?

MOTHER: You must calm down. After all, you're not to blame for everything. You don't have a reason to be afraid. She won't be able to do anything against you.

ILEANA: What do you know?

MOTHER: My dear, I don't understand you. Is there anything else? Maybe . . . perhaps you did things that I don't know . . . ?

ILEANA: Are you on her side? Could you? (*Transition.*) But I speak too much. After all you're her mother too.

MOTHER (*hurt*): How can you think that of me?

ILEANA (*energetically, upset*): Swear to me that you won't speak of this, mama, of all that you know!

MOTHER: How could I hurt you?

ILEANA: I don't know. I don't know. At times I'm a little afraid, it's true.

MOTHER: Rest.

ILEANA: Do you think that she'll speak with the director in order to take the part away from me? that she'll accuse me in public?

MOTHER: Sleep.

ILEANA: She's capable of everything. She is more holy than the Church as they say. Although she's far from being holy.

MOTHER: Forget it.

ILEANA: What else do you know about the manicurist?

MOTHER: She's my daughter too. I already told you. I couldn't hurt her.

ILEANA: Her, the favorite one!

MOTHER: She never has been. You know it well.

ILEANA: How do you expect me to love her if you never trust me? Speak. She's my sister, isn't she? I'm one of the family. I too am concerned. Is she involved in something? Hasn't she done anything serious to be sorry for? Because I'd like to help her also. Am I a stranger? Maybe it's true that she had nothing to do with that Caesar.

MOTHER: I'll never tell you anything about Silvia.

ILEANA (in a different tone): You, madam, must know all of her activities. All about her life.

MOTHER: I'll say nothing. The script is there.

ILEANA: There are things, intimate secrets that aren't stated, that are revealed in a glance, in a silence. Those secrets are the ones I want to know.

MOTHER: I can say nothing. I can only keep quiet.

ILEANA: She sticks to it! It's useless, my God. (Pause.) Do you know something about my private life?

MOTHER: To what life do you refer, miss? We actresses . . .

ILEANA: To my private life, of course . . .

MOTHER: We've just met. It's the first time that I've seen you. As you well understand . . .

ILEANA: I assure you that my private life is beyond reproach.

MOTHER: I'll speak with the manicurist.

ILEANA: She'll tell you horrible things about me. She detests me. She envies me as an actress and for what I am in real life and for the parts that they give me on the stage. She's capable of anything. When we pick our noses we always find something. It's disgusting.

MOTHER: That's bad manners, daughter. I've told you that ever since you were a little girl.

ILEANA: Everything is disgusting. It's loathsome to have things in your nose and have the need to pick it.

MOTHER: There are people who don't pick their noses. At least not in public. I've told you that's what you must do.

ILEANA: Those are the smart and nervy ones. Those who deny having had a head cold while they have their nostrils full of mucous. Like the manicurist. It's a true miracle that no one finds her out. She may have even been involved in murders and assaults. And she's probably sharpening her teeth to return again. She'll begin to denounce people and she'll return to her murderous career again. It always happens that way. . . .

MOTHER: Always? Again?

ILEANA (*abruptly*): Do you think its possible that the guillotine's made of paper?

MOTHER (*terrified*): The guillotine? What are you talking about?

ILEANA: Haven't you read the play? Toward the end, the guillotine works. Only for a minute, an instant, there at the back of the stage . . .

MOTHER: This play is terrible. I can't stand it.

ILEANA: Marie Antoinette . . . the hair loose and long . . . the head bowed. . . . It'd be an impressive ending . . .

MOTHER: Stop! Stop!

ILEANA: But have you gone mad? Do you work for free? This is a theater.

(SILVIA *and the* HAIRDRESSER *enter. The platform is lighted.*)

HAIRDRESSER: They are difficult situations, it's true.

SILVIA: I hope that you can do something.

ILEANA (*approaching*): Good afternoon. Are you the hairdresser?

HAIRDRESSER (*continuing her conversation with* SILVIA): It's a disagreeable situation, but we must face it. It's for the good of the theater. We must continue sacrificing ourselves. (*Turning violently to* ILEANA:) You must have guts to play your part. I understand that it's only a play, but there has to be something rotten in you to be able to play your part as well as you're doing. We've observed it in rehearsals.

ILEANA: You're mean, cruel, unjust. There's no word to define you.

HAIRDRESSER: Weren't you all those things when you collaborated in such a fashion with the criminals?

ILEANA: Don't you realize? Don't you know what theater is? You're confused! I'm an actress! It's a question of a part!

HAIRDRESSER: Your private life mustn't be very clean.

ILEANA: And what did you do? Did you set bombs?

HAIRDRESSER: I gave all for the fatherland. I have a red and black automobile, symbol of the revolution. Do you want a more upright position?

ILEANA: Well, on that, you aren't ahead of me. I have a red blouse and a black skirt that are symbolic too. I'll put them on and nobody will be able to deny that I'm a great revolutionary.

HAIRDRESSER: But I read my poem "The Beheaded Dove" the first day, at eight in the morning when the rebels entered the city.

ILEANA: I intend to read a similar one.

SILVIA: Would you dare?

HAIRDRESSER: Could you?

ILEANA: I interpret the parts they give me.

SILVIA: It's necessary for them to make changes in the play. It's not possible for everything to continue like this, so mixed up. Life isn't like this. Life is as clear as a bell.

ILEANA: It's better for you to shut up. Why don't you leave things as they are? Would you like your character explained? Perhaps you won't come out so well. You're playing a dangerous game. I warn you!

SILVIA: Why? I'm clean. I'm not afraid.

ILEANA: At best you have the soul of a traitor. After all, to be a traitor in thought is to be one in fact. You can be one at any moment. It's only necessary for circumstances to favor it.

SILVIA: You deserve capital punishment.

ILEANA: And don't you tremble when you say that? Don't you realize?

SILVIA: Are you trying to frighten me, to bribe my conscience?

ILEANA: It's a trap and you don't realize it. But I also can play games. I'll speak with the director and he'll clear up all of this. There's nothing sure in what you say.

SILVIA (to the MOTHER): Didn't you hear her? She hates me. She detests me. She's my greatest enemy.

MOTHER: You must calm down. Don't despair. Everything will soon change.

SILVIA: She wants to destroy me. She'll speak with the director in order to harm me. And I have no doubt that she'll do it in my private

life too. You already know it. This revolution has reached everywhere, and the opportunists and the hypocrites are also mixed in it
too, camouflaged so that no one recognizes them in the underbrush.
But I have my plans. I'm not going to let them cut off my head.

ILEANA (*frantically*): She's mistaken! She's mistaken! She's reading
my part! My God!

HAIRDRESSER: Be careful. It seems that you're becoming confused.

SILVIA: Becoming confused? I'm sure . . .

HAIRDRESSER (*apprehensively*): Life is full of dangers. We must measure our words and our acts.

SILVIA: But it isn't possible!

HAIRDRESSER: Don't you foresee the dangers? And if they succeed
in confusing you? And if they come to think that you're the other
one?

ILEANA (*thrilled, approaching the* MOTHER): Mama! Do you realize?
She's mistaken. She's confused. She plays my part. . . . Perhaps I
can be saved. . . .

MOTHER (*overwrought*): Silvia, Silvia . . .

ILEANA (*shaking her*): Mama, mama, it's me, Ileana . . .

SILVIA (*out of control, carried away by the confusion*): She's capable of anything. She's more Catholic than the Church, as they say.
Although she's far from being holy.

MOTHER (*shouting*): Forget it!

SILVIA: What else do you know about the mani . . . (*She does not
succeed in finishing the sentence. She realizes the confusion.*)

HAIRDRESSER: Be silent. . . . Be silent.

SILVIA (*scared, frantically*): The net! The net! It's a trap. It's a
damned trap. She wants to trap me like a rat. It's a shame! She's a

degenerate. They are losing us in a labyrinth. Oh, my God, how careful one must be in this world. Not a word, not a movement, not a gesture in vain. What a filthy plot . . . what dirt . . .

ILEANA: Go on, go on. I'm not to blame. You're the plotter. You're one of those who want to save themselves by destroying the rest. You're the one who came here to insult me. . . . Now, abide by the consequences. You'll see where it all will end.

HAIRDRESSER (*to* SILVIA): She knows everything.

MOTHER: Can't we live in peace? Must everyone throw the first stone?

HAIRDRESSER (*approaching the* MOTHER *as a friend*): It's true. You're right. We aren't heroes; nor are we martyrs. . . . Everything is so disappointing!

MOTHER: I always tell my daughters to pray . . .

HAIRDRESSER: You do well.

MOTHER: They fight. They kill themselves. They destroy themselves. Life isn't worth so much. You see them die, annihilate themselves, and you can't do anything. We mothers are this way. It's a disgrace. We ought to join together, form a league, a committee, something in order to keep our children from throwing stones at one another and splitting their heads. . . .

SILVIA (*smiling, to* ILEANA, *whispering, in a point of agreement*): Mothers are all alike, don't you think?

ILEANA: It's better to ignore them. They can't be helped.

MOTHER: I've suffered so much! I've cried so much! He was a young, so inexperienced, so good! At times I think I shouldn't have sent him to school. . . . His ideals! His yearnings!

HAIRDRESSER (*with alarm*): Of whom are you speaking? Did you have a son?

MOTHER (*with surprise*): A son? Did you say a son?

ILEANA: Don't pay attention to her. Mama's very old and she scarcely realizes what she says.

MOTHER: A son? A son?

ILEANA: Rest. You take the theater too much to heart.

SILVIA (*hysterically*): What are you afraid of? Let her speak. Why do you try to coerce her?

MOTHER: A son? My son, yes, my son! I've suffered so much. . . . I've suffered so much. . . . At times I didn't even want to remember him . . . his love of the . . . of the . . . it's a word that doesn't find a way out . . . his love of the . . . his death . . . his death. . . . No . . . no!

ILEANA (*passing her hand over the* MOTHER's *head*): Wake up, mama. It's a nightmare.

HAIRDRESSER: Did you have a son?

MOTHER: Sometimes, just to have him alive at my side, I'd prefer anything, anything at all, rather than his death. We mothers only have children, children, nothing else. It's difficult to think of anything else. It's hard to make our hearts see the reasons. It's so difficult. God! Children, dead children. . . .

HAIRDRESSER: And revenge? Justice . . . revenge . . .

MOTHER: Is it possible?

HAIRDRESSER: Justice will console your heart . . .

MOTHER: How? How?

ILEANA (*interrupting the sequence from the platform*): My nails . . . could you fix my nails for me? I've been waiting a while for you.

SILVIA: Customers! Always annoying and in the way!

ILEANA: And my hair? Dear, I can't go on with my hair like this.

HAIRDRESSER (*getting up*): Excuse me. We have no other recourse but to take care of her.

MOTHER (*withdrawn*): Justice . . . Revenge . . .

(*The* MOTHER *remains crestfallen. The area where she is grows dim. The action is concentrated on the platform.*)

HAIRDRESSER: I'm sorry that you have had to wait so long, but these last weeks we have had a lot of work.

ILEANA: I've decided to cut my hair.

HAIRDRESSER: Why? You have very beautiful long hair, some lovely waves . . . and these golden streaks . . .

ILEANA: They make me look like a foreigner.

HAIRDRESSER: But it looks good on you.

ILEANA: I don't want it.

HAIRDRESSER: It's a pity to cut it off. Wouldn't you prefer to have it gathered in curls at the back of your neck?

ILEANA: Please, don't insist! Oh, you hairdressers, always the same!

HAIRDRESSER: It's a shame.

ILEANA: I want to look attractive.

HAIRDRESSER (*combing* ILEANA's *hair*): Are you going to a party?

SILVIA (*maliciously*): A trial perhaps . . .

ILEANA: How do you know?

HAIRDRESSER: Have they accused you of something?

SILVIA: I understand that she had relations with Commander Camacho.

ILEANA (*upset*): That has nothing to do . . . I'm not responsible for what he did or didn't do when he wasn't with me . . .

HAIRDRESSER: Of course . . . of course . . .

SILVIA: But it's being investigated, you know; it's being investigated. Many things will come out in the open . . .

ILEANA (*with a forced laugh*): Not in my case, dear! Not in my case! In other cases, perhaps. Everything has been an error which will clear up in due time. The interrogator told me that I had nothing to fear. After all, I'm only a defenseless woman.

HAIRDRESSER: It's a pity that for nothing at all you cut your hair off.

ILEANA: Don't get upset. I also want you to dye it for me.

HAIRDRESSER: You're a beautiful natural blonde.

ILEANA: But it's no longer in fashion. Brunettes are in style.

HAIRDRESSER: I think that you've lost your mind.

ILEANA: Just the opposite.

HAIRDRESSER: And your nails? (*Sarcastically.*) Perhaps you want me to paint them green for you?

ILEANA (*with interest*): Do you have that color?

HAIRDRESSER: Don't be foolish! Of course not!

ILEANA: What a pity!

HAIRDRESSER (*annoyed*): Look, I think you'd better come shampoo your hair.

(ILEANA *and the* HAIRDRESSER *leave.* SILVIA, *upset, addresses the audience from the platform.*)

SILVIA: She's a shameless one. I don't know how they let her free. Women like that irritate me. . . . Don't they realize? She wants to transform herself. She takes advantage of the confusion of the moment and will make herself pass even for a revolutionary, if it were necessary. She is capable of anything. That rabble deserves to be killed. One shouldn't have pity on them.

(*Rapid dimming of the corner where* SILVIA *is. The area where the* MOTHER *is sitting is slowly lighted.* SILVIA *goes there and falls in the other chair.*)

SILVIA (*falling in the chair*): I'm exhausted . . .

MOTHER (*stands up, solicitously*): I'll serve your meal at once. A lot of work?

SILVIA: Now, women want to paint their fingernails green.

MOTHER: In my day . . . in my day these things didn't happen . . .

ILEANA (*from the shadows*): Do you believe it?

SILVIA: They're shameless. Now they want to pass as honest and decent.

MOTHER: You must calm yourself. Don't insist on changing the world.

ILEANA (*without being seen*): There's always something rotten in Denmark, isn't there?

SILVIA: It makes me mad, Mom. I can't stand it.

MOTHER: Don't be that way. Live and let live. Sleep. Forget it.

(ILEANA *enters. She is dressed as a servant, with an apron and a feather duster.*)

ILEANA: Caesar phoned you this morning.

SILVIA (*upset*): What are you doing here? What do you want in my house?

ILEANA: I'm the new servant.

SILVIA: Mom, explain yourself. What does all this mean?

MOTHER: You need to rest. You have too much work. What's the matter with you?

SILVIA: That woman. How did you dare hire her?

MOTHER: The servant? What's special about her? I called an agency and . . .

SILVIA: It's she, Ileana, that woman who detests me. . . . That snake . . .

ILEANA (*sarcastically*): Are you accusing me . . . ?

MOTHER: I don't understand . . .

ILEANA: She's lying, madam. I assure you. Everything has been a mistake.

SILVIA (*beginning to doubt*): Aren't you . . . ?

ILEANA: No, I'm not. (*Taking out her identification card.*) Here's my I.D. card. You've confused me with someone else.

SILVIA (*rejecting it*): It's you, it's you! I can't stand it! You've trapped me in a circle. And you're on her side. The two of you have agreed to destroy me, to annihilate me . . .

MOTHER: My dear, how can you? . . . My tears, Lord, my tears! . . . What is this? I don't understand this world. . . . It's too complicated . . .

SILVIA: Mama, mama, but don't you realize?

MOTHER: I don't know her, Silvia; I swear it to you. I don't know who that woman is.

SILVIA (*to* ILEANA): Go away from here! Leave me! Your intrigues . . . your schemes. . . . Damned woman! Aren't the crimes you have committed enough for you? Don't involve me in your dirty tricks! I'm innocent, innocent! Go away! Go away!

ILEANA (*moves away, laughing*): Caesar phoned you. Caesar. Do you remember him? Caesar, the one from the previous regime. (*She leaves.*) Caesar! Caesar!

MOTHER: What will you do with him? What have you decided?

SILVIA: Disown him.

MOTHER: But . . .

SILVIA: As if he didn't exist.

MOTHER: But he calls you . . .

SILVIA: Do you want to ruin me, harm me? I can do nothing for him. Let him leave me alone!

MOTHER: He insists. He hasn't stopped calling you.

SILVIA: Tell him that I'm not in, that I don't want to know anything. If I had what he has! But when he was in the cabinet, he gave me only the crumbs. Let him go to hell! Let him leave me in peace!

ILEANA (*crosses the stage, laughing*): Caesar. Caesar.

SILVIA: He only harms me. Let them send him to a concentration camp. It doesn't matter to me. My career, mama, my career! My honor and my career! Does he want to tear me to pieces? Does he want to drown me because he is a boat that is sinking?

MOTHER: Don't get upset, daughter. It's not so bad. (*With a certain anguish.*) After all, you don't have anything to fear, do you?

SILVIA: Of course not! I'm not going to allow him to destroy me. I'm not going to allow it. Everyone will see my upright position.

ILEANA (*crosses again, smiling*): In bed all of us are in a supine position. The bed. The toilet. We all need them. (*She leaves.*)

SILVIA: You were crazy to hire that woman. Now she knows many things, many secrets. She'll invent things. She'll go to the courts. She'll reveal all of the business of this house. She'll try to harm me, but I'll defend myself. I have connections . . .

ILEANA (*shouting from off stage*): Caesar, Caesar!

SILVIA (*shouting*): Go away! Beat it once and for all.

ILEANA (*enters. She is not wearing an apron now. She carries a small suitcase, like someone who is leaving*): I'll go, but we'll meet each other again. The world is small and keeps turning all the time.

SILVIA: I know how to defend myself.

ILEANA: I do too. (*She leaves.*)

MOTHER (*frightened. Transfigured, she stands up*): She'll return again. It's terrible what I have to say. I've an enormous lump in my throat.

SILVIA (*falls in the chair*): I'm exhausted. These rehearsals are tiring.

MOTHER: Don't you realize . . . ?

SILVIA: Why don't you rest a little?

MOTHER: If I only could. . . . That man, Caesar, did he ever prompt you to do anything really bad?

SILVIA: Caesar? But of whom are you speaking?

MOTHER: Did he perhaps say things to you that he shouldn't have . . . ? A small indiscretion and perhaps . . .

SILVIA: You too? But of what are you speaking?

MOTHER: Was he . . . simply . . . your lover?

SILVIA: But what are you up to ? I've come to detest this part! So many slanders have been woven around it . . . !

MOTHER (*desperately*): But someone was to blame. Someone betrayed him miserably and took him to his death. Someone's guilty of his misfortune and of my sorrows . . .

SILVIA (*frightened*): Not I, not I! . . . Perhaps that woman, that Ileana. . . . She has always seemed suspicious to me. Don't forget that she was involved with Commander Camacho. And Camacho was an important person in the Secret Police; isn't that so? Then . . .

MOTHER: But don't you realize that that's no solution for me? On the contrary, it's a punishment, a deep grief that's tearing me apart.

SILVIA: Maybe she's guilty.

MOTHER: It is a nightmare. When they gave me the script they told me that I was Ileana's mother and yours. It was somewhat contradictory, but I was ready to accept the part. But now, when I realize . . . now they demand too much of me . . .

SILVIA: You torment yourself uselessly. After all, the guillotine is cardboard.

MOTHER: You're blind. You don't realize. I'm his mother! I already told you. It's a trap.

SILVIA: His?

MOTHER: Yes, his! And he's dead and my heart grieves and writhes and cries out madly, like in a nightmare. I don't want to hear it. I want a deep silence and not to know anything.

SILVIA: You exaggerate, as usual.

MOTHER: I can't avoid remembering him. . . . He too is my child. Why do I have to be his mother? His voice . . . his smile . . . his words. . . . But I want all of that to move away from me. . . . I suffer too much. . . . It's too painful. . . . Why have they given me this part? God, God, I don't want to be the mother of all of you!

SILVIA: You're talking nonsense. You can't continue working. This role has shattered your nerves.

MOTHER: Will I ever be really certain of your innocence?

SILVIA: But would you think me capable of a base action? I'm a decent woman. . . .

MOTHER: I'm glad, I'm glad that you are innocent. . . . But I can't forget his mutilated body . . . his death. . . .

SILVIA (*surprised, frightened*): You're confused and complicate things. That role doesn't suit you.

ILEANA (*appears hotheaded and wrathful*): There's your work! There's the result of your efforts! Keep on stirring things up. . . . We'll smother in the stench. . . .

MOTHER: Will you both dare to deny me? Is it that I, who have suffered so much, am not going to be sure of having carried him in my womb, of having loved him, of having seen him dead, of having heard my own voice choked in my throat?

SILVIA (*uncertain, worried, trying to be persuasive*): It's a farce. It's a farce.

MOTHER (*firmly*): My son is dead. That's not a farce.

ILEANA: We must give her a sedative. Don't you love your mother? You have driven her to the verge of madness. (*Solicitously, to the* MOTHER:) Sleep, mama. Rest. Forget . . .

MOTHER: I can neither sleep nor forget. He was my son, wasn't he? His young body mutilated, covered with wounds and blood . . .

ILEANA: It's a nightmare, mama. Sleep, rest . . .

MOTHER: Don't try to intimidate me. The guilty ones must pay. Only that way, perhaps, I'll rest. It was she, no doubt, who denounced him. He confided too much in that woman. He revealed to her all of his plans. That woman! That woman!

SILVIA: That woman?

MOTHER: Yes, a woman. It was a woman who tore him from my side. I remember her voice. She used to call him on the telephone.

SILVIA: If you heard her voice, would you be able to recognize her?

ILEANA (*to* SILVIA): Don't be stupid.

MOTHER: Yes, I remember her voice. I'll never be able to forget it.

SILVIA (*to* ILEANA): I'll know how to defend myself from all this. You'll see. You won't be able to escape.

MOTHER: It was realized only too late who she was.

SILVIA (*enthusiastically*): You ... you're much more than Camacho's mistress. We'll see how the guilty will come to the light. (*To the* MOTHER:) Don't worry, mama. Everything will clear up. I'll help you. (*Referring to* ILEANA:) I always disliked her.

ILEANA (*angered*): You have no evidence against me. No one has. They can prove nothing against me.

SILVIA: Confess! Confess!

ILEANA: I've nothing to confess. I've nothing to repent.

MOTHER: The voice ... that voice ...

SILVIA: Do you recognize it?

ILEANA (*kneeling*): Mama, don't you realize?

MOTHER: He too was my child.

SILVIA: Then you can recognize her voice, can't you?

MOTHER: How could I forget it?

ILEANA (*laughing hysterically, maddened*): Caesar! Caesar!

MOTHER: That voice ... I remember it ...

SILVIA (*with annoyance*): Why are you bringing up that gossip about Caesar now?

MOTHER (*referring to* SILVIA): Yes, it's she. Mr. Commissioner, I'm sure. I haven't the slightest doubt.

SILVIA (*to* ILEANA): I'm not involved in any crookedness. No one knows anything about me.

MOTHER: Justice! It's necessary that justice be done for my dead son.

SILVIA (*to the* MOTHER, *calming her*): It will be done, ma'am, it will be done. The revolution, ma'am, punishes as it should. You can be sure of it. Its justice is infallible.

MOTHER (*referring to* SILVIA): The same voice. I remember it. It's that one.

SILVIA (*transition. Fearful*): It's I, mama, Silvia. Your daughter Silvia. It's my voice, mama . . .

MOTHER (*moving about the stage as if she were blindly pursuing the voice*): That voice . . . that voice. . . . Don't let her escape. . . . It's she . . .

ILEANA: Cold! Hot! Caesar! Innocent! Cold! Hot!

MOTHER: It's she . . . it's she . . .

SILVIA (*overwhelmed*): She has lost her mind. She has gone mad. My poor mother! We must shut her up. (*To* ILEANA:) Don't you think so, sister?

ILEANA (*singing*): *Here's the prisoner we have caught! My fair lady!*

SILVIA: But have you also gone mad?

MOTHER: It's she, Mr. Commissioner, I recognize her. I would recognize her among thousands.

SILVIA: It is I, your daughter, your own daughter . . .

MOTHER: A daughter? No, I don't remember her. . . . You're mistaken. It's about a son and he's dead.

SILVIA: Crazy . . . crazy . . .

MOTHER: Your voice . . .

ILEANA: Cold! Lukewarm! Warm! You're burning!

MOTHER: Your voice . . . I'm sure . . .

ILEANA (*falling, weakened, in a chair*): It's already too late . . .

MOTHER: Yes, I'm sure. . . . It's her voice . . .

(*The stage grows dim. Little by little the roll of drums is heard. The spectral scenery of the background with the guillotine is lighted. Some shadows are projected on that background, shadows of soldiers beating drums. The stage is lighted again. The chairs have disappeared.* ILEANA *and* SILVIA, *ghostlike, appear in long tunics with their hair loose.*)

ILEANA (*taking a step forward*): To die . . .

SILVIA (*taking a step back, horrified*): To die? Is it certain?

ILEANA (*taking a step forward*): Innocent? Guilty?

SILVIA (*backward*): I'm innocent! I've done nothing!

ILEANA (*forward*): You lie. We've all done something.

SILVIA (*now at the back, beside the guillotine*): It isn't true, it isn't true. It's she. Don't take me! Don't kill me! Stop! Stop! (*She falls.*)

ILEANA (*sarcastically. She turns and applauds*): Magnificent! Stupendous! Without a doubt you're the better actress. They'll give you the critic's award! (*Approaching* SILVIA, *she takes her by the hand and drags her to the front of the stage.*) Come, come. You have to receive the flowers, hear the applause. . . . (*Bowing.*) Do it this way. . . . A slight gesture. (*Joking.*) But if you prefer the socialist style, of course! (*Applauding.*) Applaud! Applaud!

SILVIA (*letting go, backing away*): How can you keep on with your sarcasm? Don't you realize that we're going to die.

ILEANA (*transition. Superficially*): But, do you take it seriously too, like that ridiculous mother of ours who weeps for us and for him? Look, I still intend to work in television.

SILVIA: Are you sure that the guillotine is paper?

ILEANA (*with a certain sarcasm*): Marie Antoinette . . . your hair back, loose and long. . . . The strange, overwhelming blade beneath the sun. . . . (*She laughs.*) You're an imaginative one! It would be an impressive ending. . . .

(*The sound of the drums becomes louder. The stage front becomes dark. Silhouettes of the two characters are seen among the shadows. They stand out against the back of the stage, together with the dazzling presence of the guillotine. The* MOTHER *appears.*)

ILEANA: Caesar! Caesar!

MOTHER (*accusingly*): She's the one, Mr. Commissioner. She's the one.

SILVIA: You mean Commander Camacho! Commander Camacho!

MOTHER (*accusingly*): It's she, Mr. Commissioner. It's she.

ILEANA AND SILVIA: No, no! Help! I'm innocent!

MOTHER (*falling on her knees*): My son, my poor dead son! Finally, Finally!

(*The stage goes dim. Suddenly, a scream after a quiet pause. The lights now fall on stage front, where the* MOTHER *still is.* ILEANA *and* SILVIA *are not there. The* HAIRDRESSER *enters.*)

HAIRDRESSER: Help! Help! The blood! My God! What is this? It can't be! They're mistaken!

MOTHER: Silvia! Ileana! My daughters! It has been a trap. It wasn't a nightmare.

HAIRDRESSER: A doctor, a doctor! Isn't there a doctor who can save them?

MOTHER: My daughters! Speak! Where are they?

HAIRDRESSER: Blood! They're dying! They're losing blood!

MOTHER: The guillotine!

HAIRDRESSER: Yes, it is true. The guillotine! They've fooled us!

Everything was true. Blood runs again as before, much more than before. It wasn't a comedy.

MOTHER: But you told me, you swore to me that it was made of paper. My poor, my poor and adored son dead! And now them, my daughters, my poor, poor daughters dead. . . . There's no pity, there's no pity, there's no mercy. . . .

HAIRDRESSER: It was a trap. It was a paper trap prepared by those damned gods. . . .

MOTHER: Can I no longer save them . . . ?

HAIRDRESSER: It's too late. . . . They're dead. . . .

MOTHER (*her voice suffocated*): The guillotine . . . the guillotine. . . .

CURTAIN

❧ Dialogues

Luisa Josefina Hernández

(Mexico)

Luisa Josefina Hernández

Luisa Josefina Hernández studied dramatic theory and composition under the legendary Rodolfo Usigli at the Universidad Nacional Autónoma, as did a number of the outstanding contemporary Mexican dramatists. Born in 1928, she received her degree in literature from the same university. On two occasions she received fellowships from the Centro Mexicano de Escritores. At another time a grant from the Rockefeller Foundation enabled her to study in the United States. When her former mentor, Usigli, took leave of his university classes to serve his country as a diplomat, Luisa Josefina Hernández replaced him. ■ Her first drama, *Aguardiente de caña* (1950), took first prize in the Fiestas de Primavera competition in 1951. Other works of hers were also singled out for honors. In 1954 *Botica Modelo* (1951) received the prize offered by the newspaper *El Nacional*. Three years later *Los frutos caídos* (1955) captured a prize in the Festival Dramático of the Instituto Nacional de Bellas Artes. In addition, she has written *Los sordomudos* (1950), *La corona del ángel* (1951), *Afuera llueve* (1952), *La llave del cielo* (1954), *Los duendes* (1958), and *Arpas blancas, conejos dorados* (1959). *Los huéspedes reales* (1956), considered her best play, reaches an almost classic intensity in its treatment of incest. ■ Although she is best known for careful psychological studies of family conflicts, she has more recently turned to epic devices, as in the historical play *La paz ficticia* (1960). This work was followed by *Escándalo en Puerto Santo* and *Historia de un anillo*, both in 1961. Her latest titles include *La fiesta del mulato* (1966) and *El urogallo* (1970). ■ In *La calle de la gran ocasión* (1962), Luisa Josefina Hernández presents nineteen short dialogues, three of them found in this collection. Each dialogue is a minor masterpiece of character delineation, capturing fleeting but profound revelations of the human situation.

Dialogues

1. Florinda and Don Gonzalo

Felice sono nella tua cortesia
Michelangelo Buonarroti, *Sonetti*

FLORINDA: My name's Florinda and I'm a dressmaker.

DON GONZALO: I'm pleased to meet you, miss. What can I do for you?

FLORINDA: Ah, nothing. Mrs., I'm a widow. You must know that for more than a year I've been living opposite here, in that blue house. I had a quiet moment and I decided to cross over and visit you.

DON GONZALO: Do you want . . . to sit down?

FLORINDA: No, it isn't necessary. The fact is that I said to myself: "Don Gonzalo spends every afternoon seated in the doorway reading. Perhaps a bit of conversation might suit him."

DON GONZALO: I'm grateful to you.

FLORINDA: No. I was dying to speak with you, because I too feel lonely.

DON GONZALO: Don't you have anyone?

FLORINDA: Two women who help me: one who takes care of the house and the other, a seamstress, who helps with the sewing. But in the afternoon, when they finish working, they go with their families. I certainly don't have a family.

DON GONZALO: I have my brother and his wife, but they have too many things to do to sit down and talk with me. I understand. . . . I'm somewhat of a nuisance.

FLORINDA: Don't say that!

DON GONZALO: I'm not complaining. It's useless to complain of things which have no remedy. I try to bother them as little as possible. I spend all morning in my room and finally at this time, I come near the door. That's always entertaining. One sees the cars, the people . . .

FLORINDA: But you don't see anything! All the time I've been living across the street, I've never noticed you raise your eyes from your book.

DON GONZALO: Perhaps. Sometimes I don't feel any curiosity.

FLORINDA: Wrong. Curiosity is the source of many discoveries.

DON GONZALO: Like which ones, for example?

FLORINDA: All inventions, like the sewing machine. What would I do without it?

DON GONZALO: Do you work a lot?

FLORINDA: Several hours a day. When some holiday draws near I work more, even at night. But it doesn't matter. I earn more than I need to live on.

DON GONZALO: That feeling must be very satisfying. I haven't earned a penny in my life.

FLORINDA: But it brings loneliness.

DON GONZALO: Why don't you get married again?

FLORINDA: I've had two suitors, but I don't like them. We widows are difficult to please. We know a great deal about life.

DON GONZALO: I imagine so. Once, I was in love, when I was very young. A friend of the family who used to come every day . . . we would speak of many things. . . . But, what could only be expected, happened.

FLORINDA: And what was that?

DON GONZALO: Her parents found out and they advised her to marry another fellow. She resisted for some time, but she ended by accepting him and I agreed. What kind of life would she have had at my side?

FLORINDA: If the two of you loved one another, a lifetime of love.

DON GONZALO: You're very romantic . . . Florinda.

FLORINDA: For a widow, yes.

DON GONZALO: Girls want to have a good time, go out, have friends. I'm used to being a burden, but I couldn't have endured being one for my own wife.

FLORINDA: You're very proud, and in order to be happy it's necessary to have humility.

DON GONZALO: Everything is learned too late. There's always time to think; however, to act there's but a moment, only one.

FLORINDA: Don't be a pessimist, Don Gonzalo. Life is long.

DON GONZALO: That's no consolation for me.

FLORINDA: You're so handsome, Don Gonzalo!

DON GONZALO: . . .

FLORINDA: Pardon me if I've bothered you. That wasn't my intention. I wouldn't want you to consider it all as lost and to speak without hope. Life . . . life's miraculous.

DON GONZALO: Do you believe that?

FLORINDA: Yes. Of course one has to do something on his part. Don Gonzalo, . . . I decided to come to see you after thinking it over for many months. The first time that it occurred to me, I thought that I'd never dare. Then, as time passed I began getting used to the idea, so much so that this morning, I now see it as the most natural thing in the world.

DON GONZALO: Among neighbors, a visit doesn't deserve so many doubts.

FLORINDA: A simple visit, no. But it's a question of something uncommon.

DON GONZALO: What could it be?

FLORINDA: A proposition. I wanted to ask you if you'd like to come to live with me. I'd take care of you, and you on your part would keep me company and we'd have conversations when you desired to speak and when not, I'd resign myself to your handsome presence.

DON GONZALO: Then it's . . . a proposal of marriage?

FLORINDA: Only in case you wanted to see it that way. I'll be satisfied just with your coming to my house.

DON GONZALO: You're . . . very touching. Remember that I can't help you in anything and that on the other hand I'd give a lot of bother.

FLORINDA: I've already told you that I earn more money than I spend and that I've time to spare. Do you accept, Don Gonzalo?

DON GONZALO: Tell me, what made you think of it?

FLORINDA: From looking at you so much. I used to look at you from behind the window blinds and then I began to dream of you and to imagine you so clearly that I almost knew what you were thinking about when you were distracted from your book or when you sighed. Then I opened the window and I sat down there to sew, but you didn't seem to see me and I became very impatient.

DON GONZALO: I did see you.

FLORINDA: Ah!

DON GONZALO: Only . . . how dare I?

FLORINDA: That had also occurred to me. I thought, "If he has seen me, all the more reason for me to go and speak to him."

DON GONZALO: Won't you be sorry?

FLORINDA: I, Don Gonzalo, am very determined.

DON GONZALO: I'd like to ask one thing of you.

FLORINDA: Whatever you wish.

DON GONZALO: That you marry me.

FLORINDA: Thank you very much, Don Gonzalo. I'll be happy to marry you.

DON GONZALO: And, when . . . when are you coming for me?

FLORINDA: Well, now. The truth is that I was coming now to pick you up, and I intended to return home with you.

DON GONZALO: Now? Right now?

FLORINDA: As it's a matter of only crossing the street and that's so easy. . . .

DON GONZALO: And, the wedding?

FLORINDA: We'll arrange it there.

DON GONZALO: And, my family?

FLORINDA: We'll inform them later . . . as it's just across the street.

DON GONZALO: In everything you're a woman of understanding. Let's go.

FLORINDA: Let's go.

DON GONZALO: Be careful in getting off the sidewalk because this wheelchair is getting shakier by the minute.

FLORINDA: Don't worry, Don Gonzalo. Close your eyes and think that the street is a river. I'll let you know when we reach the other shore.

12. *Dolores and Alberto Suárez*

Never believe anyone happy who depends on happiness.
Lucious Annaeus Seneca, *Letters to Lucilius*

DOLORES: Although you don't answer me when I greet you, nor ever speak, nor do you seem to look at anything or anyone, I'm determined to talk with you.

A. SUÁREZ: . . .

DOLORES: In the first place, although instead of being in jail you're in this hospital, I don't believe that you're crazy.

A. SUÁREZ: . . .

DOLORES: In the second place, I know that you've looked at me and, to your shame, from the day you arrived. When they brought you in bleeding on the stretcher, I was there and I felt you looking at me. I wasn't horrified. Nor did I have pity on you.

A. SUÁREZ: . . .

DOLORES: There was no reason to have pity on you, after what had happened. To kill your wife with one shot. Your wife who was so pretty, so good, and who in all innocence was cutting flowers in the garden, just because you were drunk. A pretty story and an excellent recommendation. Of course then you tried to commit suicide . . . and you didn't succeed. Although you almost did.

A. SUÁREZ: . . .

DOLORES: Other people do inspire pity; you don't. Sometimes when the wounded arrive, tears overwhelm me or I become frightened. But you're like the fakir who came to give an exhibition and set up his tent in the main square. He said that he was going to be stretched out for thirty days with his hands pierced by nails. That fakir was very handsome, but he died of a heart attack on the twenty-eighth day. . . .

And he really did die, when the whole town had already paid to see him. They erected a very elegant monument to him.

A. SUÁREZ: . . .

DOLORES: But you didn't even die. You remained here seated without speaking, imagining that you were in jail. But you're not, Mr. Suárez. You're in a sanitarium, and I'm the director's daughter and you're looking at me.

A. SUÁREZ: . . .

DOLORES: You, like the fakir, have also had your publicity. Don't tell me that you didn't realize that they had written a song about you that goes: "Alberto Suárez did kill his poor wife Mariquita who never did any wrong, in the garden of his house. . . ." Don't make such a face.

A. SUÁREZ: . . .

DOLORES: At one time, people offered us money to see you. Now you're out of style. It was then that it occurred to me that it was a great advantage to live here and be able to see you for nothing, Mr. Suárez . . .

A. SUÁREZ: . . .

DOLORES: Now that, because of the accident they've had me in bed, I've had the opportunity to look at you more closely. I'm speaking to you because now I'm on the road to recovery and soon I won't be able to approach you without awakening suspicions. My mother already warned me that you're a furious madman. But I'm not afraid of you, Mr. Suárez. Ever since the lightning bolt struck my foot I understood that I was, as it were, shielded and that nothing in the world could harm me, not even your madness. If it had occurred to you to shoot me, instead of killing me, the shot would have only burned a lock of my hair. You already see that the lightning didn't even leave me lame. Besides, there's something the two of us know from experience: it isn't so easy to die.

A. SUÁREZ: . . .

DOLORES: You live by your sorrow, according to you. I live by luck, and I've decided that I do so for some very special reason. Since my experience with the lightning, everything is changed. I was going to marry the notary's son, that boy who used to come to see me every afternoon, but I finally finished with him. That Dolores who could have made him happy is long dead. The lightning killed her because she was like everybody else. Now the other one remains, and that other one is so put to the test, so much above common ordinary happiness, that she can aspire to marry you.

A. SUÁREZ: . . .

DOLORES: You've placed your hand over your heart! Be careful for what happened to the fakir might also happen to you, and this isn't the right time.

A. SUÁREZ: . . .

DOLORES: And you've a tear, there at the edge of your eyes. Now it slid away. Don't cry, Mr. Suárez, for you don't allow me to think calmly.

A. SUÁREZ: . . .

DOLORES: You've been here for three years and according to the judge, you'll remain another four. And that's because they believe that you aren't right in the head. But I've done nothing; I'm very sane and I almost never leave here because this is my home. Therefore, I know that the hospital isn't such a bad place to live. Especially if one has all the things here that one goes out to look for along the street. You could help my father in running the hospital. He's old now and you're an accountant. You could be useful in many ways. You'd speak again and then, maybe, you'd even laugh from time to time.

A. SUÁREZ: . . .

DOLORES: You could also marry me, if it pleased you.

A. SUÁREZ: . . .

DOLORES: What way is that of showing that you agree? They're looking at us, Mr. Suárez. I tell you that they're looking at us.

A. SUÁREZ: . . .

DOLORES: It's better this way. From afar, for now. And from today on, let's live until someone shoots us with a bullet, or a bolt of lightning strikes us.

15. Dragon and Martha

*And she led him to
a neighboring town.
There, the mob killed
him with sticks and
stones.*
Jacobus de Varagine, *The Golden Legend*

DRAGON: I can't even imagine how you dared to enter this forest. I don't know what to tell you because you're no doubt informed of the fate that befalls those who dare. Either you don't appreciate life or you're carelessness itself. Didn't anyone warn you of what could happen to you?

MARTHA: They told me something.

DRAGON: Nevertheless, here you are. Prepare yourself. Think your last thought and try to make it worthwhile; perhaps you'll thus reconcile yourself to the idea of what will happen to you.

MARTHA: I'm thinking it.

DRAGON: I suppose you know that I'm going to devour you.

MARTHA: Do you like to devour people?

DRAGON: It's immaterial to me, but that's the way I live. I like to live.

MARTHA: I also like to live.

DRAGON: It doesn't seem so. Are you ready now?

MARTHA: Yes.

DRAGON: How calmly you say it!

MARTHA: What do you expect?

DRAGON: Nothing. I don't know. Tell me what you thought of.

MARTHA: Of you. Intensely.

DRAGON: Of me! What did you think of me?

MARTHA: That at last I'd met you. I've been thinking for many years. First, I thought that the best thing that could happen to me was to find a shepherd—one who would stretch out in the sun and would have tangled hair that smelled of the country. Then, a little later, I thought of a prince with eyes like two violets and black hair . . . and a sword that would sparkle with dazzling flashes. But when I found out that in the forest there was a dragon, half man, half fish, with shining wings and a tongue of fire, I could think only of him. Night after night, I've thought of you. Until today in the late afternoon, I decided to come in search of you. I've seen you and I'm satisfied. . . . You're more handsome than I thought.

DRAGON: And you're ready to allow yourself to be devoured. Don't you feel afraid?

MARTHA: Very afraid. But as you said before, in substance, it's immaterial to me. I did it in order to live. Your wings are iridescent and the fire from your tongue is blue.

DRAGON: You scare me. At night I can scarcely rest thinking that soon a squadron of armed young men will come ready to tear me to pieces. I live on the watch . . . and now a young woman appears wrapped in a tunic which she holds up with a belt made of string. . . . Won't I have been for you the monster who apparently exists in all dreams?

MARTHA: You're a dream. A very beautiful dream. And you, weren't you thinking of anyone?

DRAGON: Creatures like me have hallucinations. I see green sirens and sea gulls and women with tails. Sometimes, a queen with a high crown, barbarous and bejeweled.

MARTHA: What a pity that I'm not a queen!

DRAGON: You're not a hallucination.

MARTHA: It's a pity. Devour me.

DRAGON: Don't be in a hurry. That long blonde hair is . . . is it soft?

MARTHA: Touch it.

DRAGON: I'd burn you. My blue fire consumes everything it touches.

MARTHA: That's the way extraordinary things are. They can be possessed but they never touch us. Someday, a squadron of armed young men is going to come to look for you and . . .

DRAGON: I'll wipe them out. It's written that no one will destroy me, apart from me myself. Do you know something? I know the taste of flesh, but not the touch.

MARTHA: Flesh is smooth, soft, warm. Imagine it to yourself; it's like the wind at midnight. It's like when your forest falls silent, but you know still that it lives and that it caresses you. Devour me.

DRAGON: No.

MARTHA: I won't be able to return to my home. They forbade me from entering the forest, and when I did, I rushed to a great adventure. How could I return? Could I live here?

DRAGON: You'd eat nuts and mushrooms. The forest is as you say, warm and welcoming. In some places yellow flowers grow. You'd bathe in the stream. . . . I'd like to touch you and I can't.

MARTHA: Devour me.

DRAGON: No! No!

MARTHA: What's happening to you?

DRAGON: My fate is fulfilled and I'm happy.

MARTHA: I don't know what you're saying.

DRAGON: I'm saying the same thing that you thought before entering the forest. The same thing that you've repeated so many times. Destroy me. I do it in order to live. Obey me.

MARTHA: What do you want me to do?

DRAGON: Untie the cord that you wear at your waist. Tie it around my neck and take me with you wherever you go.

MARTHA: I obey.

CURTAIN

﹏ The Forceps

Román Chalbaud

(Venezuela)

Román Chalbaud

Born in Mérida, Venezuela, in 1931, Román Chalbaud turned to the theater at a very young age. He received a thorough training for the stage from the Spanish director Alberto de Paz y Mateos, leader of an innovative dramatic group in Caracas in the early 1950s. One of Venezuela's foremost directors today, Chalbaud has also worked as an actor. He founded El Nuevo Grupo, an experimental group which has brought the works of outstanding national and foreign dramatists to the attention of the Venezuelan theater-going public. ■ *Los adolescentes* (1951), his first play, won the Premio Ateneo de Caracas in 1952. *Muros horizontales* (1953) and *Caín adolescente* (1955), both of which deal with the conflicts facing the Venezuelans who come from the country to live in the city, followed. *Requiem para un eclipse* (1958), dealing with an oedipal situation, recalls T. S. Eliot and Christopher Fry in its exclusive use of verse. This piece is particularly significant because it contains those features which will become the trademark of Chalbaud's mature art—his concept of action as a ritual interplay of man's passions and thoughts, unconventional characters and subjects chosen to awaken the audience to the truth, and a subtle manipulation of symbolic meanings. ■ His later plays include *Cantata para chirinos* (1960), *Sagrado y obsceno* (1961) (the staging of which constituted a major scandal and which, paradoxically, was a striking audience success), *Café y orquídeas* (1962), *La quema de Judas* (1964), *Días de poder* (1965), *Los ángeles terribles* (1967), and *El pez que fuma* (1969). Most critics concur that Chalbaud's best play to date is *Los ángeles terribles*. ■ *The Forceps* (*Las pinzas*) was first performed in 1962 as part of an experiment which involved two other playwrights—José Ignacio Cabrujas and Isaac Chocrón. Each one of the three undertook the writing of a one-act piece evolving from given initial lines. The result, entitled *Triángulo*, was presented on the same bill. In a series of cruel games, *The Forceps* touches upon modern man's inability to assume moral responsibility for his acts.

The Forceps

Characters
WOMAN
FIRST MAN
SECOND MAN
Time: Present
Place: The World
Setting: Three doors—center, left, and right

(*The stage is empty. The* WOMAN *enters through the door at the right. She goes to stage center.*)

WOMAN: Here we are.

(*Through the left door the* FIRST MAN *enters. He takes a position at the side of the* WOMAN *and speaks.*)

FIRST MAN: Is that true?

WOMAN: Does it surprise you?

FIRST MAN: I believe that we were more.

WOMAN: It isn't a question of quantity.

FIRST MAN: Are we going to wait for him?

WOMAN: We are here.

FIRST MAN: It seems to me that I've been doing the same thing for many years.

WOMAN: And it's the first time that we're going to do it.

FIRST MAN: If you're not careful you'll do it three times in a row.

WOMAN: I don't understand what you're saying.

FIRST MAN: Understand! Understand! You don't understand! You never have understood.

WOMAN: I understand something. That's why I'm here.

FIRST MAN: And does it seem to you that it's necessary to understand something in order to be here? I wouldn't say so.

WOMAN: You contradict yourself. Are we going to do it, or aren't we?

FIRST MAN: Little by little we're going to do it . . . (*Laughs*) or undo it. . . .

WOMAN: All of this turns my stomach.

FIRST MAN: I don't feel that way. Do you know what I feel?

WOMAN: Of course I know. You feel enthusiasm, ardor, that optimism that's eating you.

FIRST MAN: Do you see? Again! You think you know me, everyone thinks they know me! You attribute feelings and sensations to me. . . . No! The only thing that concerns me is that he gets here, that . . . (*He disappears through the door at the left.*)

WOMAN: He'll get here. At any moment he'll be here. (*Pause.*) Don't laugh, I beg you.

VOICE OF FIRST MAN: Laugh? At whom? At him . . . or at you?

WOMAN: When one talks with you, it's difficult to know.

FIRST MAN (*enters, as he finishes dressing himself as an archbishop*): Now, for example, at whom am I laughing?

(*He puts on the miter. Through the door at stage center, the SECOND MAN enters wearing glasses, humble, timid. He carries a man's old suit on a hanger. The WOMAN and the FIRST MAN stare at him. The SECOND MAN stares intently and bewilderedly at the FIRST MAN. He draws closer. He kneels.*)

SECOND MAN: Monsignor, Monsignor . . . forgive me!

FIRST MAN: Have you sinned a lot?

SECOND MAN: I've arrived late.

FIRST MAN. I forgive you.

SECOND MAN (*toward the* WOMAN): Allow me, ma'am, to kiss your hand also. You're good. You've kept your promise. (*He kisses her hand.*)

WOMAN: What did you think? That you weren't going to find us here?

FIRST MAN: You, yes! But him! It's incredible! You've succeeded in getting him to come. You're a good woman!

SECOND MAN: Here it is. The suit . . .

WOMAN: Give it to me.

SECOND MAN: The bowling pin . . . the gift . . . and the letter. Where do I put them?

(*He gives the suit to the* WOMAN. *She takes it. He searches in his pockets and takes out the mentioned objects.*)

FIRST MAN: There, on the floor.

SECOND MAN: Here?

FIRST MAN: Yes, there . . . ˙

SECOND MAN (*puts the objects on the floor and remains with the letter in his hand, trembling*): Monsignor, here are his things, his knickknacks. That was his suit. He died in it. He was wearing it when he felt a strong pain in his stomach.

FIRST MAN: How many days did he suffer?

SECOND MAN: One day.

FIRST MAN: One day only?

SECOND MAN: No. I'm lying—two days, two days. The first day he grabbed his stomach through that suit and went to see the doctor. They took an X ray.

FIRST MAN: Were they there?

SECOND MAN: Yes, they were. Inside. Some large and shiny silver forceps. They had operated on him six months before. They left the forceps inside of him. That's why he suffered and he'd grab his stomach through that suit. He suffered that day. On the following day, they operated on him in order to take ou the object. He died naked on the operating table. I picked up his suit, his last suit.

FIRST MAN: Put it on.

SECOND MAN: What are you saying, Monsignor?

FIRST MAN: Put it on.

SECOND MAN: Here?

FIRST MAN: Yes, here.

SECOND MAN: In front of her?

FIRST MAN: She won't look.

SECOND MAN: She has eyes.

FIRST MAN: God won't allow it. For a moment she'll be without them.

(*The* WOMAN *gives him the suit. The* SECOND MAN *takes it. He undresses. He stands in his underwear, and then he starts to put on the suit. While he does so, the* SECOND MAN *speaks.*)

SECOND MAN: Can I tell you the rest?

FIRST MAN: Do.

SECOND MAN (*still dressing*): Do you see that bowling pin? My brother had a friend who used to go to the bowling alley. It was an elegant place for nice people with money. My brother dreamed of being able to go to the bowling alley and to throw a big, heavy black ball of wood against thousands of pins . . . (*Picks up the pin from the floor*) like this one. . . . One day . . . (*Plays with the pin, then juggles it*) my brother's friend got drunk, and my brother convinced him to take him to the bowling alley. My brother was smart. He could convince anyone by the way he talked. His friend took him to the bowling alley, and my brother bowled forty-eight hours without stopping. . . . He had never bowled, but nevertheless he knocked down all the pins. He'd grab the big ball, throw it, and . . . bam! bam! bam! . . . The same thing time after time for forty-eight hours, without eating, without sleeping. . . .

WOMAN: Then, your brother already had the forceps in his stomach?

SECOND MAN (*frightened*): I hadn't thought of that. (*Transition.*) But . . . look . . . look, this pin was the only one that my brother couldn't knock down . . . in the last hour . . . the forty-eighth hour. . . . He knocked down all of the pins . . . except this one. He took it with him. . . .

FIRST MAN: He took it with him . . . ?

SECOND MAN: He stole it. And he always carried it in his pockets or played with it in the air, as I am doing now. . . . Oh, excuse me, I haven't finished dressing myself! Can I explain the rest?

FIRST MAN: Do it all at the same time.

SECOND MAN: You believe me, Monsignor. Isn't it true that you believe me?

FIRST MAN: Yes, my son.

SECOND MAN: Oh, the letter! I'd forgotten the letter. Look, this is the letter. The last one my brother wrote. It seems he had a hunch that he had a foreign object inside his body. Do you want me to read it to you?

FIRST MAN: Allow me. (*He takes the envelope from him, removes the letter from the envelope, and looks at it. The* SECOND MAN *does not take his eyes from him. The* FIRST MAN *glances from the letter to the* SECOND MAN.) Continue dressing. Don't worry.

SECOND MAN: Yes, Monsignor. (*He continues dressing.*)

FIRST MAN: I don't understand the writing . . .

SECOND MAN: I'll read . . .

FIRST MAN (*stares at the* SECOND MAN. *The* SECOND MAN, *timid, stops looking at him and continues dressing. The* FIRST MAN *speaks to the* WOMAN): You, read it.

WOMAN (*takes the letter, reads to herself, and then speaks*): Babylon, March 14.

SECOND MAN (*laughs nervously and finishes dressing*): My brother was that way. Babylon. One had to know him. He'd always date a letter from a distant city. He used to say that geography doesn't exist. For him, this city was all the cities.

WOMAN (*reading*): Babylon, March 14 . . . Dear Brother . . .

SECOND MAN: It's addressed to me, to me, to me, to his only brother. . . . It was the only letter that he wrote to me . . . , the only one. . . . (*He weeps.*)

FIRST MAN: Don't cry.

SECOND MAN: Let me cry, Monsignor. Let me cry. Even if it's for just a little while.

FIRST MAN: All right, but just for a little while.

SECOND MAN (*weeps briefly, and then speaks*): Isn't it true that tears help? I feel clean . . . , as if I'd taken a bath. . . . You understand me, don't you, Monsignor?

FIRST MAN: God understands you.

SECOND MAN: And you? What about you?

WOMAN: Tell him yes.

FIRST MAN (*after hesitating*): All right. I say that I understand you.

SECOND MAN (*falls on bended knee*): Thank you, thank you, Monsignor.

FIRST MAN (*to the* WOMAN): Continue.

WOMAN (*reading*): Babylon, March 14 . . . Dear Brother . . . Tomorrow they'll operate on me . . .

SECOND MAN: He wrote that letter the first day of the pain—two hours after they took his X ray.

FIRST MAN (*brusquely*): Keep quiet!

SECOND MAN: Pardon, Monsignor.

WOMAN: Shall I continue?

FIRST MAN: Continue . . .

WOMAN (*reading*): Babylon, March 14. Dear Brother . . . Tomorrow they'll operate on me. Two hours ago the doctor looked at me through his X rays. . . . I weighed more . . . , a whole pound more . . .

SECOND MAN: Poor soul. A pound more. Of course, the forceps. . . . He was fat. He weighed enough. He laughed about his weight, and how he used to eat. He used to eat in order to weigh more. . . . Look how badly his suit fits me. . . . He was fat, very fat. He ate, and he ate . . . and besides a pound of forceps. . . . It was enough! It was too much!

FIRST MAN: Don't interrupt.

SECOND MAN: I'd like you to understand me.

FIRST MAN: As long as you keep on this way, I can't understand. . . . If you interrupt . . .

SECOND MAN (*puting his index finger to his lips*): Sh . . . sh . . . ,

I'll be quiet. . . . I promise not to interrupt you anymore. . . . I want you to understand . . .

FIRST MAN (*shouting*): Stop! (*To the* WOMAN:) Continue.

WOMAN (*reading*): Babylon . . . March 14 . . . Dear Brother . . .

FIRST MAN (*approaches her, confidentially*): It isn't necessary for you to begin again each time . . .

WOMAN: It's that . . .

FIRST MAN: It's nothing. . . . I won't stand it. . . . Do you understand? I can't take any more of this.

WOMAN: Me either, but . . . let's go on. We have to go on. . . .

FIRST MAN: But don't begin again. . . . Continue . . . , continue . . .

WOMAN: We're here. It is necessary to go on.

FIRST MAN (*moves away from her. The* SECOND MAN *remains at stage center. Again in his role of archbishop*): All right, continue . . .

WOMAN (*cannot help laughing—like someone who commits a prank in a very serious moment and in spite of herself*): Babylon . . . March 14 . . . Dear Brother . . .

FIRST MAN (*losing control*): No! No!

(*He pounces upon her and takes the letter from her and tears it. The pieces flutter over the* SECOND MAN.)

WOMAN: No!

SECOND MAN: No! What have you done, Monsignor? You aren't making fun of me, are you? No, it can't be! Pardon, Monsignor! But . . . what have you done? It was his letter . . . , my brother's letter . . . the only one that he wrote to me . . . Monsignor! (*The* FIRST MAN *kneels beside the* SECOND MAN *who takes him by the shoulders.*) No, Monsignor, don't kneel; you can't kneel; not you. . . . If you tore the letter, it's for a reason. . . . You're right. . . . Get up . . . get up . . .

FIRST MAN: Listen to me! Look at me; look at me! What do you believe of me?

SECOND MAN: You know . . . I don't believe anything . . . I mean, yes, I believe in everything, in God, in you. . . . I believe, I believe, I believe. (*He beats his breast. The* FIRST MAN *laughs.*) Are you laughing at me?

FIRST MAN (*getting up*): From happiness. I'm happy to have met a man like you . . .

SECOND MAN: Like me?

FIRST MAN: Pure, good, happy . . .

SECOND MAN: I'm not happy . . .

FIRST MAN: Happy! . . . You're happy . . . when you cry and you believe, you're happy. You're pure, you're holy, you're happy . . .

SECOND MAN: If you say so . . . , but I'm confused . . .

WOMAN: Confused? Did you say confused?

SECOND MAN (*as if realizing now what he has said*): Yes, confused . . .

WOMAN: I'd like to speak with him alone for a moment . . .

FIRST MAN: I understand. I want to rest. I'm going to wash my hands. (*He leaves by the left door. Pause.*)

SECOND MAN (*gets up. In another voice. He ceases to be timid and hesitant. He says to her convincingly*): And now? Is it the right time?

WOMAN (*taking him to the extreme right*): Careful. He can hear.

SECOND MAN: What'll we do?

WOMAN: Wait. It isn't the right time.

SECOND MAN: Does he think that I believe he's an archbishop?

WOMAN: He believes it.

SECOND MAN: Are you sure? Hasn't he realized?

WOMAN: Impossible.

SECOND MAN: He behaves in a strange way. I'd have been able to realize . . .

WOMAN: He's nervous.

SECOND MAN: Where did you get the costume? From a theater wardrobe?

WOMAN: No. It's authentic. He stole it himself from the holy chapel.

SECOND MAN: How did you convince him?

WOMAN: I told him that he was going to perform an extraordinary experiment.

SECOND MAN: Are you sure that he doesn't suspect?

WOMAN: No, no . . .

SECOND MAN: What kind of man is he?

WOMAN: Cold, cerebral.

SECOND MAN: A bad man?

WOMAN: Sort of a bad man.

SECOND MAN: I have to kill him, don't I? I have to kill him.

WOMAN: He killed your brother, didn't he?

SECOND MAN: Yes.

WOMAN: What's the matter? Are you getting cold feet?

SECOND MAN: No, not at all. I want to play a little more with him. Play, play, play. . . . He played with my brother's life. He left those forceps in his poor stomach . . .

WOMAN: Sh . . . sh. He's coming.

(*The* FIRST MAN *enters. He stares at them. He goes to the* WOMAN.)

FIRST MAN: I want to speak with you alone . . .

SECOND MAN (*returning to his initial role*): No, Monsignor, no . . . I don't want to separate myself from you . . . don't go away.

FIRST MAN: I'm not going to leave . . .

SECOND MAN: The gift is missing. . . . I didn't tell you about the gift. . . . (*He picks it up from the floor.*) Look what a nice package. . . . Look at that red bow and that pretty colored paper. . . . Do you know who gave it to me?

FIRST MAN: Your brother . . .

SECOND MAN: Exactly . . . , my brother. . . . Why did you tear the letter? You'd have learned. . . . At the end he told me . . . , I know it by heart: Dear brother, this is my posthumous gift . . .

FIRST MAN: Haven't you ever opened it?

SECOND MAN: Of course, I've opened it a hundred and one times; but each time I wrap it again with great care and make the bow exactly like my brother did . . . , because he made it himself. . . . Look how nice!

FIRST MAN: Why don't you open it now?

SECOND MAN: I don't dare. Now I don't dare.

FIRST MAN: Give it to me. I'll do it. It's necessary for me to see it, isn't it? If you don't show me everything, if you don't tell me everything, I won't be able to speak to you about the spiritual destiny of your brother. And that's what you want to find out, isn't it?

SECOND MAN: Yes . . .

FIRST MAN: Then, give me the package.

SECOND MAN: Yes, Monsignor. (*He gives it to him.*)

FIRST MAN (*while he opens it delicately*): From all of these proofs, from all of your narrations, the truth will come forth. Your brother died March 14 . . .

SECOND MAN: March 15 . . .

FIRST MAN: Yes, it's true, March 15. . . . But it's very possible that he hasn't gone directly to heaven . . .

FIRST MAN: What are you saying, Monsignor? It's not possible! It's not possible! No!

FIRST MAN: Don't despair. There are antechambers.

SECOND MAN: He was good, pure, holy . . .

FIRST MAN: Like you.

SECOND MAN: Better than I. . . . He was a fat man. . . . He was better than I. . . . You must assure me that my brother's in heaven. . . . I couldn't live . . . I couldn't live . . . , if I found out that he's . . .

FIRST MAN (*after finishing unwrapping the small box, he removes the gift, some forceps*): . . . in hell.

SECOND MAN: No! In hell, no!

FIRST MAN: These are the forceps, aren't they?

SECOND MAN: Do you realize? All of that inside his stomach. . . . A pound of forceps. . . . How they shine! What they must weigh! They are poisoned!

FIRST MAN: In his stomach. . . . And the doctor? . . .

SECOND MAN (*upset*): What doctor?

FIRST MAN: The doctor who left the forceps inside your brother's stomach . . .

SECOND MAN: Ah! the doctor, the surgeon? . . .

FIRST MAN: That one!

SECOND MAN: Well yes . . . that one . . . , I don't know . . .

FIRST MAN: You don't know?

SECOND MAN: My brother was operated on six months ago. He had those forceps inside of him for six months. But on that date I wasn't in the city.

FIRST MAN: Where were you?

SECOND MAN: In the country, the country . . .

FIRST MAN: What were you doing in the country?

SECOND MAN: I was sick also. . . .

FIRST MAN: What did you have?

SECOND MAN: Tuberculosis, Monsignor.

FIRST MAN: Perfect.

SECOND MAN: In what way perfect?

FIRST MAN: Perfect. Everything's perfect. Your story is perfect.

SECOND MAN: It isn't a story. It's true. It's my story. My brother's.

FIRST MAN: Perfect.

SECOND MAN: The police are looking for the surgeon.

FIRST MAN: What are they going to do to him?

SECOND MAN: I don't know. For a crime, eight or ten years. For a robbery, one or two years. For having left some forceps inside my brother's stomach . . . , I don't know . . . , I don't know.

FIRST MAN: Are you going to keep them always?

SECOND MAN: Always. I'd like to swallow them. And die as he did. . . . But before I do I need to know . . .

FIRST MAN: Yes, heaven or hell. . . . It's difficult!

SECOND MAN: Difficult? For you? No! For you it's not difficult, Monsignor.

FIRST MAN: May God enlighten me!

SECOND MAN: You are eternally enlightened.

FIRST MAN: I'd like to think for a moment alone . . .

SECOND MAN: Alone?

FIRST MAN (*to the* WOMAN): Take him inside! Give him something to eat. He looks hungry. (*Pause.*) Don't you hear me? Take him.

WOMAN (*to the* SECOND MAN): Come with me. That way . . .

(*She indicates the door to the right. The* SECOND MAN *goes first.*)

FIRST MAN (*to the* WOMAN, *as she is about to leave, in a low rapid, convincing voice*): You! Come back! Quickly!

(*She looks at him, makes an affirmative gesture, and leaves.*)

FIRST MAN (*alone, he wanders about nervously. Suddenly he begins to laugh and laugh. He realizes that they can hear him and he stops. The* WOMAN *enters.*) Does he know?

WOMAN: Yes.

FIRST MAN: For sure? Doesn't he believe that I'm an archbishop? A real archbishop?

WOMAN: Fool. Even if you were, you wouldn't look like an archbishop.

FIRST MAN: Then, he knows?

WOMAN: Yes!

FIRST MAN: He knows it and he believes it! It's going to be the happiest day of his life. Do you know what has occurred to me?

WOMAN: What?

FIRST MAN: We're going to go further.

WOMAN: Further?

FIRST MAN: You get dressed too!

WOMAN: As an archbishop?

FIRST MAN: No, as the brother.

WOMAN: As the brother? How?

FIRST MAN: With his own suit. (*He takes the* SECOND MAN's *suit from the floor.*) Take it. Dress yourself.

WOMAN: It turns my stomach. You're laughing. At heart you're laughing.

FIRST MAN: And him? Doesn't he turn your stomach?

WOMAN: No. He's pitiful. He only thinks of his dead brother. He does everything for his dead brother.

FIRST MAN: What do the dead matter? Let's continue the game. Now we'll be the archbishop and the brother.

WOMAN: And why not the doctor and the brother?

FIRST MAN: The doctor and the brother?

WOMAN: Take off that outfit.

FIRST MAN: I?

WOMAN: Take it off! If you take it off, I'll dress as the brother.

FIRST MAN: All right.

(*The* FIRST MAN *takes off the archbishop's suit and throws the pieces offstage through the door at the left. The* WOMAN *puts the* SECOND MAN's *suit on over her dress.*)

WOMAN: It's not going to do. He's skinnier than I.

FIRST MAN: Very much skinnier. He's the skinniest of the three.

WOMAN: The only skinny one. It doesn't fit me. It's impossible.

FIRST MAN: Force it. Force the material. Pull your stomach in, fast. You have to get into those pants.

WOMAN: It's very tight on me. Don't laugh. Do I look like the brother?

FIRST MAN: Not in the least. Did I look like an archbishop? Not at all, either. Do I look like a doctor now?

WOMAN: Yes, you look like the doctor who killed the brother. You've the face of a murderer. On that point you look like the doctor. And I? What do I look like to you? Where's the hat?

FIRST MAN (*picking it up*): Take it.

WOMAN (*putting it on*): I should lie down, shouldn't I?

FIRST MAN: Yes, and I'll take the forceps and I'll stoop down and I'll place them on your stomach. That's what he ought to see.

WOMAN: Will you have the nerve to do it?

FIRST MAN: Of course! If not, we've wasted our time.

WOMAN: We need something.

FIRST MAN: What?

WOMAN: To call him.

FIRST MAN: I'll do it. . . . Lie down. (*The* WOMAN *obeys. She lies down on the floor, in the center of the stage. The* FIRST MAN *calls in the mellifluous voice commonly used in children's theater.*) Come . . . , you can come. . . . Come. . . . (*Silence.*) What can be happening?

WOMAN: Isn't he coming?

FIRST MAN: Come, dear friend. . . . Come . . . , we're waiting for you. . . .

(*Silence.*)

WOMAN: Nothing?

FIRST MAN: I'm going to look for him . . .

SECOND MAN (*bounds through the door at the left, dressed as an archbishop*): It isn't necessary! Here I am! (*The* FIRST MAN *steps back, frightened. The* WOMAN *sits up surprised.*) Surprise! Isn't it so? Surprise! But, who are we?

WOMAN (*lying down again*): Your brother's dead . . . , your brother's dead. . . . He's playing with you. . . . (*Desperate for everything to end.*) He's the doctor, the doctor who killed your brother. Look at him. He has the forceps in his hand. It is he. . . . I'm your dead brother.

SECOND MAN: But I'm playing with him. . . . (*He pounces upon the* FIRST MAN.) Give me those forceps . . .

FIRST MAN: No . . .

SECOND MAN: Give me those forceps.

FIRST MAN: No.

SECOND MAN: Give me those forceps. (*In a silent struggle he succeeds in taking them from the* FIRST MAN.) Look at them. One day you left them in my brother's stomach. Now I'm going to leave them also in your stomach. . . . Do you see? (*He sticks the forceps on him.*) Look, in your stomach, in your stomach . . .

(*The* FIRST MAN *falls. The* SECOND MAN *steps back. The forceps fall to the floor. The* WOMAN *sits up.*)

WOMAN: Finally! Finally! You've killed him. You're happy! You've avenged your brother!

(*The* SECOND MAN *gives a cry as though scared by what he has done, and flees through the center door.*)

WOMAN (*stares, surprised. She waits a moment and then speaks*): You can get up. He's gone now.

FIRST MAN: Everything has turned out well, hasn't it? He ought to be happy. He believes he killed the doctor. We've done a good deed, haven't we?

WOMAN: No, I don't know. We shouldn't have lent ourselves to this game.

FIRST MAN: Are you sorry?

WOMAN: Yes, he gave a shout and he left. He'll believe himself a murderer. From today on he'll believe himself a murderer.

FIRST MAN: But he's a happy man.

WOMAN: Careful. There he comes. Lie down again. Pretend you're dead. (*The* SECOND MAN *enters running through the center door.*) What's the matter?

SECOND MAN: A policeman is chasing me.

WOMAN: For the crime?

SECOND MAN: No, on account of these clothes. (*He takes off the archbishop's vestments.*) He realized that I'm not an archbishop. I'm not an archbishop. But he's dead, isn't he. A dead man. . . . Is it true that I killed him?

WOMAN: With the forceps!

SECOND MAN: You shouldn't have let me do it . . .

WOMAN: You wanted to kill him, avenge yourself . . .

SECOND MAN: You shouldn't have let me.

WOMAN: I don't understand you . . .

SECOND MAN: You're the ones who don't understand me. . . . You lent yourselves to a game that went as far as death. . . . Yes, I wanted to kill him, but you shouldn't have let me. . . . Give me my suit . . . that's my suit. . . . I want to take off this one of my brother's . . .

(*Both undress in order to exchange suits.*)

WOMAN: Tell me . . . if a miracle were to happen, if he were to return to life, would you like it?

SECOND MAN: Yes, I'd like it.

WOMAN: Even if he were the doctor, the real one?

SECOND MAN: Even if he were the doctor, the real one.

WOMAN: Why?

SECOND MAN: I was desperate. Desperation always carries us very far. Now I'd like to retrace my steps to be at peace with myself, not to have killed anyone.

WOMAN: Well, you've killed no one.

SECOND MAN: What?

WOMAN: You've killed no one. (*To the* FIRST MAN:) Get up. (*The* FIRST MAN *gets up.*) Do you see? You haven't killed anyone.

SECOND MAN (*looks serene. He now has his original suit on. He takes the big suit. He hangs it on the hanger. He picks up the objects, and before leaving as he came, he says*): I've killed no one. I don't want to kill anyone, but my brother died.

WOMAN (*shouting*): What is it you want then?

SECOND MAN (*leaving*): You can't understand.

(*The* WOMAN *and the* FIRST MAN *look at each other as though feeling guilty.*)

WOMAN: The two of us went too far.

FIRST MAN: We've failed.

WOMAN: We played a game, and you were cruel.

FIRST MAN: We all played the game. We didn't understand.

WOMAN: Disgust. Disgust. That's what I feel.

FIRST MAN: All right! Stop!

WOMAN: If we'd understood him . . . , really understood . . .

CURTAIN

ᥰ Ladies at Play

Julio Matas

(Cuba)

Julio Matas

Born in Havana in 1931, Julio Matas attended the Seminar of Dramatic Arts at the University of Havana while working there for a degree in law. After his graduation, he founded the experimental theater group Arena which staged, under his direction, contemporary plays by both foreign and Cuban authors. Arena's presentation of *The Bald Soprano* in 1956, probably the first Ionesco play produced in Latin America, had a tremendous impact on Havana's theatrical world. Matas took an active part in the Cuban theater in the capacity of actor and director until his exile early in 1965. ■ *Retrato de tiempo* (1959), a collection of poems, first brought him to the attention of the Cuban public. He was closely associated with the review *Lunes de Revolución* to which he contributed original poems, texts, and translations. A collection of his short stories, *Catálogo de imprevistos*, was published in 1963 by Ediciones R, an outgrowth of *Lunes de Revolución*. A second volume of short stories appeared in 1971. ■ In 1964 his three-act play, *La crónica y el suceso*, dealing with the conflict between reality and its artistic representation, was published by Ediciones R. Due to Matas's decision to leave Cuba shortly after its publication, this play did not find its way to the stage. To date it remains unperformed. In addition to the play included in this collection, he has completed two others—*El cambio* and *Diálogo de Poeta y Máximo*. At present he is working on an adaptation for the stage of one of his short stories, "Historia de entreguerras." ■ *Ladies at Play* (*Juego de damas*) treats one of the major concerns of Matas's art—the maddening effect that frustrations in realizing long-cherished dreams can have on human life. A macabre sort of humor allows for a break in tension in the play. The author sees this work as a catharsis for him as well as for the reader or spectator.

Ladies at Play

Characters

ERNESTINA
CELESTE
FLORANGEL

Setting: An extremely modest living room, in an apartment building that was respectable forty years ago. Dark walls that have not been painted in a long time. To the left, a narrow window. To the right, stage rear, an opening covered by a curtain and, stage front, a closed door. Old furniture, at the point of collapse; faded upholstery on the two armchairs and the sofa. A pianola by the window. Small tables, a floor lamp more ornamental than practical. Bibelots, vases, small bottles.

(On stage, anxious, ERNESTINA and CELESTE, of indeterminate ages, somewhere between fifty and seventy. Dressed in their best regalia, very made-up and adorned. They give the impression of carnivallike grotesque figures. ERNESTINA, leaning out of the window, looks below. CELESTE contemplates the furniture and ornaments, adjusting something here and there.)

ERNESTINA: Here she comes! The chauffeur is opening the car door for her. *(Pause.)* She got out already. *(Pause.)* Now she's entering the building. *(Moving away from the window.)* Composure, Celeste.

(The two become very dignified, very stiff, laughing at each other.)

CELESTE: Who will open the door for her?

ERNESTINA: The two of us will.

(They remain expectant, listening. First the creaking of the elevator cables is heard, and at last the noise of its iron doors as they open.

Footsteps. The bell rings, very harshly. ERNESTINA *and* CELESTE *advance toward the door, slowly, majestically.* ERNESTINA *opens it.* FLORANGEL *appears, a contemporary of the two, expensively dressed, but in good taste. She has the haughty air that a more-than-comfortable life usually gives.*)

FLORANGEL (*sincerely, moved*): Tina! Cel!

ERNESTINA AND CELESTE (*at the same time*): Flor, dear, honey, how are things? (*The tone is cloying, affected.*)

ERNESTINA: But, come in, dear, and excuse the house. . . . You know by now that what little we have is offered sincerely.

CELESTE: Sit here (*Taking her to the sofa*) for it's the most comfortable.

(FLORANGEL *and* CELESTE, *on the sofa;* ERNESTINA, *in the armchair.*)

FLORANGEL: For heaven's sake, don't bother at all for me. Why it's like being in my old home. (*She becomes very moved, her voice chokes.*)

ERNESTINA: When we were neighbors, do you remember, Cel?

(*She makes a face at the latter who responds with another one, even more exaggerated.* FLORANGEL *is busy taking from her purse a handkerchief, which she then uses for her nose.*)

CELESTE: Of course! And how could we forget Lucy, so sweet and good. May God have her in His glory. (*Motion with her hand to* ERNESTINA.)

FLORANGEL: Poor mama, how happy she would be if she could see me now. (*The emotion becomes more intense, and she is now weeping openly.*)

ERNESTINA: Poor Lucy. (*A scoffing gesture which, naturally,* FLORANGEL *does not see.*)

CELESTE: But, dear, don't carry on so. Do you want me to bring you something to drink?

FLORANGEL: No, no, thank you, it's nothing. It's already over.

ERNESTINA: Cel, bring her a glass of water. (*Signals and winks.*)

CELESTE: Right away. Wouldn't a little tonic be better?

FLORANGEL (*making a motion of refusal with her hand, she hiccoughs*): Uh, uh.

(CELESTE *separates the curtains and leaves.*)

ERNESTINA (*sitting next to her on the sofa*): Calm yourself, dear, you shouldn't carry on that way. Lucy's looking at you from heaven, and what she sees should make her very happy.

FLORANGEL: How good you are, Tina! I'm better now. Don't pay attention to me; it's the effect of returning here after so many years.

ERNESTINA: When Cel saw the notice in the newspaper, she said to me (*Imitates* CELESTE), "How good it would be to see Flora again, but since she's an important person now, she probably won't want to see us." "But dear," I said to her, "there's no better and less affected person than Flor. I'll call her and that's that." It was a lot of trouble to find your number. However, you can't imagine how well the operator behaved when I explained the situation. Well, at last, you're here, as I intended and Cel and I wanted. And how well you look! The years don't pass by for you. (*She takes* FLORANGEL's *hand.*)

FLORANGEL: Don't exaggerate.

ERNESTINA: No, it's true. Of course you haven't had the troubles we've had. That is, after you married the American. You know that we rely on papa's pension.

FLORANGEL: Pardon me, I don't want to offend, but you already know that whatever you need . . .

ERNESTINA: The idea! No. Thank God, we manage well. We don't lack the necessities. . . . (*She sighs.*) Well, and you've traveled half the world . . . haven't you?

FLORANGEL: Yes . . . of course, at the beginning it was to some extent an obligation. (*Somewhat upset.*) My husband, as you know, was a diplomat. When he retired he couldn't get used to the sedentary life, so he bought a yacht, and off we went.

ERNESTINA: I've always dreamed of traveling. But at this point you already know which trip awaits me.

FLORANGEL: Ah, dear, don't be so glum. Look, between my weeping and your remarks we're spoiling this moment, which is more properly for celebrating. (*She tries to laugh.*)

CELESTE (*entering with a tray of sweets and cold drinks*): That's it, we have to celebrate this get-together. (*After she puts the tray on the table, she leaves and returns at once with some small dishes. While she serves the sweets and passes them with the drinks, she continues.*) Do you remember when we celebrated my engagement, just like now? Of course, it was mama who served. And in that armchair, he sat, so blond, so handsome, devouring me with his eyes. I was there where Flor is and Tina where she is now and Flor . . . where was Flor? Where were you? Do you remember?

FLORANGEL: Uh, I don't remember that I was here. . . . Was I here?

ERNESTINA: You arrived a little later.

FLORANGEL: Ah, did I?

ERNESTINA (*firmly, seriously*): Yes.

CELESTE: He was telling me, in that broken Spanish of his that was so funny, that if we were in his country, they would have already left us alone . . . and that here on the sofa (*Laughing with frightened modesty*) . . . he would kiss me until he'd left me breathless. . . . Mama looked at him severely. Just then papa came in and he got up and approached him and they walked together to the window . . .

ERNESTINA: Then the bell rang. It was Flor and Lucy. Flor was dazzling with her jewel-encrusted headband Theda Bara–style, which
Amelia Sorck, that actress who used to live in the building, had lent
her. Do you remember?

FLORANGEL (*trying to change the theme*): Yes, yes, Amelia Sorck. She
was French, or Belgian, wasn't she? A lovely girl. Although the gos-
sips said that she danced the fan dance. I never believed it. She was
very refined and her mother accompanied her everywhere. Where is
she?

CELESTE: Under the ground. (*Crudely.*) Her pimp killed her years
ago, here in the building. He threw her down the elevator shaft.

FLORANGEL: God! How horrible!... (*Without knowing what to say:*)
The man must still be in jail.

ERNESTINA: No, the thing appeared to be an accident.

FLORANGEL: And how do you know...?

CELESTE: Because we saw it all through the keyhole.

FLORANGEL: But, why didn't you speak?

CELESTE: And, what for? Didn't she ask for it?

ERNESTINA: Because she was a...

FLORANGEL: But... well... a crime (*Confused*)... wasn't it?

ERNESTINA: Well, it all depends on the way one looks at things, right,
Cel?

CELESTE (*somberly*): That's the way it is.

FLORANGEL (*with feigned vivacity*): These sweets are delicious. Did
you make them, Cel?

CELESTE: Mama's recipe, of course.

FLORANGEL: Exquisite.

ERNESTINA: That's the very thing you used to say about mama's sweets. The day of Cel's engagement, you went up to mama and you embraced her and you kissed her, saying (*Imitating* FLORANGEL:) "Exquisite, Cheché, exquisite. With this recipe. any man would surrender."

CELESTE (*with reticence*): My fiancé surrendered to them.

ERNESTINA (*with irony*): Until he stuffed himself and got weary of so many sweets.

CELESTE (*rapidly*): You're cruel, Tina. You like to rub salt in a wound.

ERNESTINA (*rapidly*): You know that I like the truth above all. To call a spade a spade. Isn't that true, Flor?

FLORANGEL: Yes . . . yes. . . . But . . .

ERNESTINA: But nothing. Do you know the game of naked truth?

FLORANGEL: No . . . I've never played it.

ERNESTINA: We play it often. It's a good outlet. It keeps us more and more united. We've played it for several years now.

CELESTE: Although I usually end by being a little offended. You already know that I'm sentimental.

ERNESTINA: Sentimental. Isn't that what Flor called you when she explained herself to you afterward . . . ?

CELESTE: I think so. Wasn't that the word, Flor?

FLORANGEL: The word? No . . . I don't remember.

ERNESTINA: There's no need to rush. Shortly, we'll be remembering everything.

CELESTE: No. We must go one step at a time. But, Flor, aren't you uncomfortable with your hat on?

FLORANGEL: No, no, really . . . (CELESTE *tears it from her head, un-*

doing somewhat FLORANGEL's *elegant hairdo.*) . . . but no. . . . (FLOR-
ANGEL, *baffled, puts her hands to her head, while* CELESTE *tosses the
hat to* ERNESTINA *who catches it with the grace of a professional
catcher.* FLORANGEL *laughs as if it were a joke.*) You're the same mischievous little girls.

ERNESTINA: Mischievous, yes. Little girls, no. Old, very old, dodder-
ing old women. (*She puts on the hat suddenly and makes a pleasing,
very 1920ish grimace.*) But spry, still spry. . . . Look.

(*She makes a sign to* CELESTE *who goes to the pianola and plays a
Charleston.* ERNESTINA *dances grotesquely.* FLORANGEL *stands up,
somewhat frightened and, not knowing what to do or to say, applauds when the dance ends.* ERNESTINA *takes two or three bows
and lets herself fall into the armchair, breathing noisily between
shouts of pleasure.*)

CELESTE (*laughing*): Like in the good old days, Flor!

FLORANGEL (*laughs, nervously*): You bet. . . . Well, it seems that I
have to go now. . . . I have other visits . . . as you can well imagine. . . .
After so many years . . .

ERNESTINA (*jumping up*): What? You're going already? By no means,
love. This is an afternoon for the great remembrances of youth.
There's so much we need to remember. . . . Or do you find it incon-
venient to share these memories with us?

(*She advances threateningly toward* FLORANGEL, *who takes a step
backward and stumbles, falling onto the sofa in a not-too-dignified
manner.*)

CELESTE (*running to the sofa*): Flor! Have you hurt yourself? (*She
caresses her head so roughly that she completely undoes her hairdo.*)

FLORANGEL: Ouch! What are you doing? Are you crazy? (*She looks
with fear alternately at* ERNESTINA *and* CELESTE.)

ERNESTINA (*conciliatorily, tenderly*): But, my dear, what's the matter with you? (*She sits down at her side.*) Don't our jokes please you any longer? Do you remember how we used to play slapstick? And how our mothers got furious? Once I remember that Lucy, to intimidate us, called the police. (*She laughs.*)

FLORANGEL (*recovering herself, as if she were following the joke*): Yes, and the policeman ended by entering into the game, and afterward he accompanied us as far as the entrance when we went to the movies. . . . And the day you disguised yourself as Valentino and forced Cheché to dance the tango? (*She laughs.*)

CELESTE: How well he danced the tango!

FLORANGEL: Valentino?

CELESTE: No, him. (*She looks at* FLORANGEL *knowingly.* FLORANGEL *lowers her eyes.*) He had a way of looking at me, while he held me tightly by the waist, that made me dizzy. And when he breathed deeply his mustache trembled as if it were the down of a golden bird. Oh, I'm ridiculous, but the fact is that I was so much in love. . . . And the things that he whispered in my ear: "Honey," "Sweetheart," "Doll." . . . And to think that he fell in love with me the day when that flowerpot fell on his head as he passed beneath the window. "Angels' hands," he said to me when I had finished fixing him up. (*She cries and laughs at the same time.*)

FLORANGEL (*seriously*): You haven't forgotten anything.

CELESTE (*bitterly*): Nothing. (*Transition.*) I was so happy.

ERNESTINA: And everything was already arranged for you to keep on being happy. Papa was convinced that you'd go abroad. Then, the official engagement . . .

CELESTE: The engagement. . . . (*To* FLORANGEL:) When you arrived he didn't see you. He was speaking with papa. I brought you up to him and he looked at you as if he hadn't seen you before, with that Theda Bara headband that you had. And it gave me a chill. Papa took me by the arm and took me aside to give me the advice that he used to give me when he drank too much. I didn't hear what he was saying. I felt as if something had been torn from inside me, and I had to smile and answer when I really wanted to shout and cry. . . . When I returned, you were still looking at each other without speaking. . . . It was a matter of a few minutes and, nevertheless, it was too late for me. But I went up to you and I took him by the arm and I made him walk around the room with me. (*She walks as she talks.*) But he no longer looked at me. Or he looked at me without seeing me, which is still worse. Ha! (*She is in back of* FLORANGEL *and she caresses her head lovingly.*) That's the way he caressed me. That's the way he probably caressed you, isn't it?

FLORANGEL (*standing up*): For God's sake, this is becoming unbearable, Celeste!

CELESTE: And do you know how unbearable all of that became for me? Did you bother about me at any time after your dirty trick?

FLORANGEL: Things are as they are. I don't deserve these reproaches. . . . And even less after so many years.

ERNESTINA (*with the face of a madwoman*): Celeste was shut up. (FLORANGEL *makes a gesture of astonishment.*) Crazy . . . or whatever. Later mama followed her. I haven't told you that she died in an insane asylum. (*Transition. Feignedly happy:*) Oh, but what a way of bringing up bad memories! Cel, that'll do. You've let yourself go on enough now. Enough of the game of truth. Don't pay attention to us, Flor. You see now how much we've suffered. We must make the best of it. Let's forget sorrows. Cel, bring the bottle of wine. We're going to toast this get-together.

(*She embraces* FLORANGEL, *who, once more, falls into the trap and returns the embrace sincerely.* CELESTE, *smiling, embraces her afterward. Then she goes behind the curtain in search of the wine.*)

FLORANGEL: Before leaving, I'll have to fix myself up. I must be a mess. With these crazy games.

ERNESTINA: Don't worry. Cel will fix you. You know that she's an excellent hairdresser. As for the rest, you're fine. Don't be frightened.

CELESTE (*returning with the bottle of wine and three goblets. She fills and distributes them*): To this moment of happiness!

(*They drink.*)

ERNESTINA: Cel, you have to fix Flor's hair. Look how we've treated her. (*She takes* FLORANGEL's *hat off, and looks at it.*) Pretty hat.

FLORANGEL: Keep it if you like it.

ERNESTINA: Thanks. (*She puts it on the pianola.*)

FLORANGEL: Well, now I do think I should begin to leave . . .

ERNESTINA (*giving a signal*): . . . Cel . . .

CELESTE: Right away.

(*She goes to the door at the right. She enters and returns a moment later with a makeup case. Meanwhile* ERNESTINA, *moved, looks at* FLORANGEL *and smiles sweetly. Finally, she makes her sit down on the sofa and she sits next to her.* CELESTE *opens the makeup case and takes out a comb, cosmetics, fine brushes, etc. She spreads them out on a table near the sofa, and, while she holds the comb in a professional manner, she hands some jars and brushes to* ERNESTINA *who begins to make up* FLORANGEL. CELESTE *combs her hair.* ERNESTINA *paints her face in a grotesque manner: lips bloody, cheeks clownlike, a lot of shadow on her eyes.* FLORANGEL *tries to free herself from that torture, but the other two violently subdue her. They scarcely allow her to cry out a few protests. At the end,* FLORANGEL *has a more carnivallike aspect than* ERNESTINA *and* CELESTE. *One notices that she is both frightened and exhausted. She gets up tottering, anxious to get to the door.*)

ERNESTINA: Celeste, open the door for Flor! (CELESTE *obeys.*) And don't forget the way, Flor. (FLORANGEL *leaves.*) Celeste, the elevator!

(CELESTE *leaves behind* FLORANGEL, *moving her hands about her own head effusively.* ERNESTINA *remains standing on stage triumphantly. The doors of the elevator are heard, and, right after, a prolonged scream and a deafening noise.* CELESTE *returns smiling and goes to* ERNESTINA. *In the distance progressively intense voices and noises are heard and a little later, ambulance and police-car sirens. The two women run to the window and look out. Finally they look at one another, take each other by the hand, and, laughing, dance happily about the stage.*)

ERNESTINA: Now, to rest, Cel, at last to rest!

CELESTE: Yes, and to sleep, Tina, to sleep!

(*They laugh fiercely over the background of street noises as the curtain falls slowly.*)

CURTAIN

❦ Love Yourselves Above All Others

Jorge Díaz

(Chile)

Jorge Díaz

Born in Rosario, Argentina, in 1930, Jorge Díaz has lived in Chile since 1934. An architect and painter until 1958, he became associated with the experimental group I. C. T. U. S. of Santiago, Chile, in 1959 in the dual capacity of actor and business manager. This association marked the beginning of a brilliant dramatic career. In 1961 I. C. T. U. S. staged his first plays—*Un hombre llamado Isla*, *El cepillo de dientes*, and *Requiem por un girasol*, which were enthusiastically received by audiences and critics. *El velero en la botella* (1962), *El lugar donde mueren los mamíferos* (1963), *Variaciones para muertos de percusión* (1964), and *El nudo ciego* (1965) appeared on subsequent programs of this troupe. ■ Díaz's art, which recalls that of Beckett and Ionesco, could be classified under the comfortable label of theater of the absurd. Without denying his indebtedness to these European masters, he admits his obligation to a long tradition of the grotesque, evident in Hispanic art from the Middle Ages to our day. Such a heritage accounts in great measure for Díaz's profound originality. ■ Díaz holds very definite ideas about the social function of the theater, and these, in turn, have shaped his own dramatic art: "I feel that we live in a wrong social structure. The bourgeois world . . . provides the antidote for any action against that society. Thus, the truths presented on the stage are sometimes received by the bourgeoisie with an ironic acceptance and almost always with joy . . . I believe that the best way to make theater audiences think today is by means of laughter. Let us turn to the comic situation, then, not as a mask to conceal truth, or as a sweet to help swallow the purgative, but as that comic spirit inherent in the human condition."[1] ■ *Love Yourselves Above All Others* (*Amaos los unos sobre los otros*, 1971) is a bitter mockery of the inequitable class structures existing in many places. At the same time it is a mordant satire of the fake solutions offered by ideologists who preach from the security of lofty positions.

1. Jorge Díaz, *Teatro* (Madrid: Taurus Ediciones, 1967), p. 64.

Love Yourselves Above All Others

Characters

THE GENTLEMAN

THE LADY

PLÁCIDO

EPIFANIO

(*The* GENTLEMAN *is seated astride* PLÁCIDO *who is on all fours. The* GENTLEMAN *is dressed formally, and* PLÁCIDO *is in worn-out patched clothes. The* GENTLEMAN *is finishing delivering a speech.*)

GENTLEMAN: ". . . And to conclude, I will give a brief summary of my position which is definitive and inexorable—(*The* GENTLEMAN *totters because* PLÁCIDO *has moved.*) don't move that way, Plácido, for heaven's sake! (*Again in position*)—of my position regarding these problems which concern us all and which have gathered us here to meditate while sipping a gin and tonic. I simply say this, "Violence, opposition, answer—agreed—but within the law and the established order." . . . Any social diagnosis (of any country which is not ours, naturally) leads us to point out the urgency of a great change in its structures. . . . (PLÁCIDO, *who is tired, has leaned his body on the floor, bending his knees even more. The* GENTLEMAN *snaps his fingers automatically.* PLÁCIDO *sits up immediately.*) This change can be conceived by some as a gradual evolution of the prevailing social forms (in almost all countries, except our own, fortunately). It can also be conceived by others as a general change, profound and rapid without anesthesia, "the armed revolution," if I'm allowed a literary metaphor, but within the bounds of liberty and respect, of course. There are very intelligent friends of mine who have written very nice things on this theme. I recommend to you the work of the Count of Santillana *Revolution, Why not?* published by Charism Press.

(*The* LADY, *very elegant and bejewelled and seated in the audience, applauds enthusiastically. Her dress is not outlandish, but realistic.*)

THE LADY: Excellent, excellent! . . . Someone had to say it!

GENTLEMAN (*with a discreet bow*): Finally, the revolution can be conceived of as a change from the popular bases that may do away violently with those structures only to replace them with new ones that originate from people themselves. . . . (*The* GENTLEMAN *snaps his fingers and he gives a sign to* PLÁCIDO *who repeats in an automatic fashion the lesson learned.*)

PLÁCIDO: Only the people themselves, conscious and organized, can work the cultural change that will lead them to the conquest and enjoyment of their liberation . . .

THE LADY (*enthusiastically*): Bravo, bravo! Have him repeat it again!

PLÁCIDO (*tiredly*): It only leads can change conscious work the liberation conquest the cultural of the people rejoices in.

GENTLEMAN (*imperturbably*): This change should occur in the world before inconsistency turns, as tends to happen (in almost all countries except ours, fortunately), into frustration and violence. . . . (*The* GENTLEMAN *snaps his fingers.*)

PLÁCIDO (*obediently*): And so we, the people, are the only true victims.

GENTLEMAN: To give a rational form to so much yearning for justice is to safeguard the dignity of man on this virgin continent . . .

THE LADY: Virgin, yes, very virgin! I ought to know!

GENTLEMAN: I'm generally accustomed to finishing my speeches saying modestly, "I hope that my words at least serve to open up new channels of dialogue," the latter a brief sentence that produces a great effect. This time, however, I won't say it because I'm a masochist.

THE LADY (*entreatingly, always, from her seat in the audience*): Please, protest! . . . Please, protest! . . . Protest! . . .

GENTLEMAN (*flattered*): And now, at the request of the fervent public that is listening to me, I'm going to interrupt the definition without an ideological position—it was a question of correcting something but I don't remember what—in order to interpret the modern and witty protest song they have applauded me for at other times. (*To the audience:*) When I say, "Boo-ooo," all protest with me. (*The* GENTLEMAN *sings:*)
> How little words mean,
> boo-ooo,
> if when the wind blows
> it carries them off after it
> and only memories remain,
> boo-ooo,
> promises that flew away
> and cannot return.
> Always live with illusion
> for each day has a different color.
> Everything comes to its end.
> After a sad day
> another happy one is born.
> Searching in the trunk of memories,
> boo-ooo,
> any past time
> seems better to us.
> To glance backwards is good sometimes.
> boo-ooo.
> To look ahead
> is to live without fear.

(*The* LADY *applauds enthusiastically.*)

THE LADY: He terrifies! He really terrifies! What courage! He doesn't mince words!

GENTLEMAN: My lifelong motto has been To Call a Spade a Spade. . . . (*To the valet:*) Plácido, give me a whiskey!

(*The valet gives him a whiskey.*)

THE LADY: How he speaks! How well he speaks! Since I can't remember when, no one has asked for a whiskey that way. . . . Really, it's a wonder how he manages, isn't it? (*This last remark is addressed to some person in the audience.*)

GENTLEMAN (*taking a little red book out of his pocket*): It's very simple. On assuming office one consults this little book, and that's all!

LADY (*in a low voice*): Is it the red book of Mao?

GENTLEMAN: No, it's the *Manual of the Terminology of Development.* (*He opens it anywhere.*) If one as head of government finds that the country is on its last legs, he should say, "A realistic focus is imposed on the economic structures. . . ." If one hasn't even the least idea of what can be done, he should say, "The means will be brought together for the gradual introduction of more suitable measures. . . ." If one believes that it's desperately necessary to get dollars, he should say, "We cannot obsess ourselves with an isolationist position nor maintain ourselves aloof from the world economic reality. . . ."

THE LADY: Don't continue, don't continue! . . . It's terrible to keep on using tear gas when terminology has advanced so! . . . (*The* LADY *stands up.*) I think that I'll go now to reflect on all this at the Benefit Bridge Party in Favor of and Against the Disadvantaged.

GENTLEMAN (*gallantly and pointing to his mount*): If you want me to take you on Plácido . . .

(*The* LADY *goes to where the* GENTLEMAN *is and possibly goes up onto the stage.*)

THE LADY: Thank you, but I left mine parked in the corridor.

(*The* LADY *snaps her fingers. Immediately* EPIFANIO, *who is another poor wretch, appears on all fours.*)

GENTLEMAN: Each day it's more difficult to park them. Of course, the fact is that there are so many!

THE LADY: Too many. (*The* LADY *sits on* EPIFANIO.) In fact, these people aren't perfect. They don't have a back that supports you.

PLÁCIDO: Upon my word!

GENTLEMAN: This is what happens to me for being good and taking off his muzzle.

LADY: Ah! Yours talks.

GENTLEMAN: I taught him.

LADY: Admirable.

GENTLEMAN: And I taught him to protest also, but politely. That's why he's so proper.

LADY (*a little coquettishly*): Could you tell him to protest for me?

GENTLEMAN: I'll try. I generally kick him on the flanks. (*He kicks him.*) Plácido, protest for the lady. . . . Come now, for she's listening to you.

PLÁCIDO: Heavens! . . . Holy mackerel! Damn it! Shit! . . . Hell!

GENTLEMAN (*severely*): Plácido!

PLÁCIDO: Pardon.

GENTLEMAN (*to the* LADY): Now you see, there's no problem. Communication between the classes is harmonious and coincident with their aspirations.

LADY: In our country we form a concerned social body.

GENTLEMAN: Our grandparents said it of old, "Love yourselves above all others."

LADY (*opening her parasol*): It's true, I, for example, do my best to protect them from the sun in the summer and from the rain in the winter, while they work.

EPIFANIO: Ouch! (*Slight moan.*)

LADY: My dear Epifanio, what's wrong with you?

EPIFANIO: Nothing, miss. It is the weight of my freedom on my back.

LADY: Sh . . . easy, easy! The community watches over you.

GENTLEMAN: Now he's smiling.

LADY: It's what they call "Hispanic joy."

GENTLEMAN: What your . . . what do you call him, said . . . well . . . that! . . .

LADY: Epifanio to his close friends.

GENTLEMAN: What Epifanio said about freedom and his back sounds like a literary metaphor.

LADY: He's a poet. The other day he told me that religious freedom is wonderful for them because thanks to it they can lose their faith in many ways.

GENTLEMAN: Don't worry. They all end up playing the drum in processions.

LADY: I understand them very well. . . . I'm very broadminded. . . . And especially about freedom of expression! (*She speaks to her mount.*) Do you want to say something, Epifanio?

EPIFANIO: Yes, miss.

LADY: Speak. You know that you have complete freedom.

EPIFANIO: Yes, miss.

LADY: I'm listening to you.

EPIFANIO: Damned be the mother who bore you . . . begging your
pardon.

LADY (*happily*): Do you see? . . . Now he expressed his feelings.
Generally after expressing his feelings, he feels like singing.

EPIFANIO (*singing, while the* LADY *is still on top of him*):
  If by chance I behave well
  —friend—
  I could be capable
  later
  and even one day
  get to stand up
  and on top of another
  mount,
  Who knows!
        At your orders, sir.
        Yes, sir.
        Thank you, sir.
        Thank you, sir.
        Thank you, sir.

PLÁCIDO: Forbear and forget
  anger
  you see now that we are free
  —friend—
  and it would be pure viciousness
  to complain
  Smile at he who causes you sorrow
  and drains you
  Tomorrow perhaps they will let me
  get on top of you.
        At your orders, sir.

Yes, sir.
Thank you, sir.
Thank you, sir.
Thank you, sir.

(*The* GENTLEMAN *and the* LADY *applaud.*)

LADY: Very good, very good! . . . When they do it in "pop" they're enchanting. One forgets that they're out.

(PLÁCIDO *sneezes.*)

GENTLEMAN (*muzzles his mount as he says*): Bless you! Without a muzzle one always catches cold. According to UNESCO, the rights of man are three: "To see, to hear, and to be silent." (*Pointing to* EPIFANIO.) Does yours go without a muzzle?

LADY: Naturally! . . . That business of muzzles is just prehistoric. Haven't you read Charlie?

GENTLEMAN: Your nephew writes? . . .

LADY: No, I'm referring to Charlie Marx. He's the most neo-Christian writer to be found in the bookstores. I give Epifano paperback editions, blue penciled, of course.

GENTLEMAN: Don't tell me that he knows how to read.

LADY: The poor soul can read only with his fingers, Braille system, but don't think that he is unhappy. (*With her parasol she gives* EPIFANIO *a blow on the head.*) Do you need anything? Tell the gentleman . . .

EPIFANIO: Here where you see me, sir, I've three million red corpuscles.

LADY: And that's not all. When spring comes he has freedom to chase the females and mount them, with me on his shoulders, of course. They love to have children.

EPIFANIO (*modestly*): That's just nature, miss.

LADY (*amiably*): Of course, I say nothing. In those matters I think as Jacques Maritain, "We must make the best of it."

GENTLEMAN: That's what happens to me. There are days when I get up very much a Christian Democrat. I don't know why. On those days that business of the social question obsesses me. Without going further, this year, instead of the year-end bonus, we'll distribute kisses and embraces to our workers.

LADY: How neo-Christian you're becoming, Don Justo!

GENTLEMAN: Tricks of metabolism, I think. I'm an insatiable being in my desire to know and to understand others. (*He speaks to* EPIFANIO.) Good sir, will you permit me to do your work for just a few seconds? . . .

(*The* LADY *gets up.* EPIFANIO *stands up.*)

EPIFANIO (*fascinated, he says to* PLÁCIDO): Didn't I tell you that they'd give me a chance!

(*The* GENTLEMAN *gets down on all fours and the* LADY *sits on top of him.*)

GENTLEMAN (*sensually*): Just as I thought! It's perfectly delightful!

LADY: I understand. Frankly, if it weren't for the money, being poor wouldn't matter to me.

(*The* GENTLEMAN *stands up again.* EPIFANIO *gets down on all fours again.*)

GENTLEMAN (*to the* LADY): On that matter, you and I are completely different. I despise money. If it weren't for my principles, for the car, the chalet, the apartment at the shore, the yacht, and the convertible, on any day I'd do a foolish thing and vote for the candidates of the moderate centro-leftist party.

LADY: Speak more softly, for God's sake!

GENTLEMAN: There's no reason to hide anything from them. You've no confidence in the good will of the people. Without freedom of expression we'd be nothing.

LADY (*in a low voice*): But they're half-breeds!

GENTLEMAN: Please, dear friend, there are no inferior races, only superior ones of course! . . . (*To* PLÁCIDO *who is still muzzled:*) What do you say? . . . (PLÁCIDO, *muzzled, grunts and emits sounds. To the* LADY:) Now you've heard him.

LADY: Why does he speak that way? . . .

GENTLEMAN: He's bilingual.

LADY: Anyway, it's nice to listen to them express themselves. (*She hits* PLÁCIDO *on the head with her parasol.*) Why, you rascal, you've spent all your life protesting in silence. Admit it! . . .

(*The* GENTLEMAN *and the* LADY *sing. The poor wretches remain motionless.*)

> [Song of the Dialogue]
> This is the dialogue, friends;
> Confrontation of criteria,
> interchange of opinions,
> open disagreement.

GENTLEMAN: Speak, good fellow, I'm listening to you;
> now you see,
> your opinion is important;
> on the contrary,
> your grunts are valuable;
> also
> we should change the world's skin
> > This is the dialogue, friends.
> > (*Same as above.*)

LADY: Nuns on motorcycles
> by the hundreds

and revisionist priests
yeh-yeh.
How progressive we are!
Baby
Give me another double scotch and soda
   This is the dialogue, friends.
   (*Same as above.*)

GENTLEMAN: I'm a genuine
demo-democrat.
Pats on the back
I also give.
Sundays they see me
without a tie
and I joke with the maids
afterward.
   This is the dialogue, friends.
   (*Same as above.*)

(*Police sirens, shouts, ambulance sirens, shots, screams of a crowd
are heard.*)

LADY: My God! . . . What's happening? . . .

GENTLEMAN: I was expecting it. Right on time. And they're very
punctual. (*The* GENTLEMAN *looks toward the audience through binoculars.*)

LADY: Who?

GENTLEMAN: It's our children who are confronting the police. I've
told them a thousand times to do it at any time except this time,
which is when I go to the theater. But it's useless. (*Describing what
he sees through the binoculars:*) There's José María, the Serraldes'
son, and Manene, the daughter of the Velasco-Ansones! . . . They're
breaking the windows of the stock exchange. Her father's shouting
at them from a window. . . . Of course, he's the major stockholder!
. . . Now Claude Iturreta and Milagritos Méndez are burning a Fiat

600. . . . As soon as they finish they'll go to supper in Milagritos's father's Mercedes. She's a very cute girl, believe me.

LADY: We parents and the Mercedeses are always the ones who end up sacrificed.

GENTLEMAN: They don't feel they've accomplished anything until they knock down a policeman or throw a dean out of the window. I've offered to buy them a policeman or a dean so that they can do it without leaving the house, but they say it's not the same.

LADY: What I don't like about young people is that they're so sado-masochistic. They rub themselves with Marcuse as if he were suntan oil. But we shouldn't be bitter.

GENTLEMAN: As far as I'm concerned, I don't hate my fellow men more than my conscience allows me. (*The* GENTLEMAN *continues looking toward the audience through the binoculars.*) Does your son have long hair and a red, high-necked sweater?

LADY (*smiling*): Yes, I had it woven by a little old woman from the asylum who makes charming things with her toes . . .

GENTLEMAN: Well, if it's your son, he's taking a dreadful beating! Three demonstrators are beating him!

LADY (*in a cry*): Surely that's my Jamie! He's gotten himself in a scrape again! . . . Jamie! . . . (*She leaves calling "Jamie."*)

GENTLEMAN: Wait! . . . I have an undersecretary friend who is the friend of a friend of Commissioner Valcárcer . . . (*The* GENTLEMAN *leaves. The two poor wretches remain motionless like statues. It is evident that they have not realized that the* LADY *and* GENTLEMAN *no longer weigh upon their backs.*)

PLÁCIDO: Are you underdeveloped?

EPIFANIO: Yes, but I am much better off than before when I lived in the suburbs.

PLÁCIDO: Whose subtenant were you?

EPIFANIO: A subintendant's.

PLÁCIDO: Well, I'm going to see if I can solve my problem by speaking with an undersecretary.

EPIFANIO: But do you have some influence in the undersecretaryships?

PLÁCIDO: Not I, but I've a relative who's subinspector.

EPIFANIO: I wish I could say the same. The most distinguished relative I have is a subaltern.

PLÁCIDO: And how do you manage to exist?

EPIFANIO: You see, in a normal way.

PLÁCIDO: You probably mean subnormal.

EPIFANIO: Well, that's subjective. Subsidiary aids are always found.

PLÁCIDO: Don't underestimate the boss. He's very good, believe me. He has promised us that he'll give us the land that'll cover our grave for our very own property.

EPIFANIO: That corrects absolutely nothing. That's why we've also had an agrarian reform. Now the only landowners are the children of the old owners.

PLÁCIDO: We've improved a great deal, to tell the truth. Formerly, in addition to the master, the young lady, the young gentleman, and the mistress of the young gentleman would mount on top of us.

(*A silence. They speak without looking at one another.*)

EPIFANIO: Is he heavy for you?

PLÁCIDO: Who? . . .

EPIFANIO: The young gentleman.

PLÁCIDO: As always.

EPIFANIO: I don't know whether it's spring . . .

PLÁCIDO: What?

EPIFANIO: He seems lighter to me now.

PLÁCIDO (*looking around*): Yes, it must be the spring. (PLÁCIDO, *after a moment, looks at* EPIFANIO.) What luck you have! Your owner has gone.

EPIFANIO: What are you saying?

PLÁCIDO: That she's gone.

(EPIFANIO *looks at* PLÁCIDO *for the first time.*)

EPIFANIO: Ah, yes, your owner has left!

PLÁCIDO: Mine? . . . I'm referring to yours.

EPIFANIO: Well, it's true! Listen, then the two have left.

PLÁCIDO: Why, man, it's true!

EPIFANIO: And now, what can we do? . . .

PLÁCIDO: Nothing occurs to me. (*A long silence. Both continue on all fours, motionless and looking toward the front of the stage with a blank expression.*) There! . . . Something occurred to me.

EPIFANIO: What occurred to you?

PLÁCIDO: We can stand up.

EPIFANIO: Do you think so?

PLÁCIDO: Of course.

EPIFANIO: And what for? . . .

PLÁCIDO: For just that, to be standing.

EPIFANIO: I'm afraid . . . , but we could try.

(*A silence. Neither one of the two moves.*)

PLÁCIDO: I think that I'm going to get up.

EPIFANIO: Don't rush. Let's talk it over a little more.

(PLÁCIDO *stands up.*)

PLÁCIDO (*standing*): There!

EPIFANIO: So? . . . How does it feel?

PLÁCIDO: Well, it's not bad.

EPIFANIO: You probably exaggerate.

PLÁCIDO: Things occur to me.

EPIFANIO: What things?

PLÁCIDO: Please, . . . will you let me do it for only a brief moment? . . .

EPIFANIO: Will I let you do what? . . .

PLÁCIDO: Climb up on you.

EPIFANIO: No, I don't want to.

PLÁCIDO: Egotist!

EPIFANIO: Just because you can stand up, I can too.

PLÁCIDO: Don't do anything foolish!

EPIFANIO: I can try it, can't I? . . .

PLÁCIDO: Thirty years of carrying the masters on your back and you can't carry me a little bit.

EPIFANIO: The masters' behinds are different. Everyone knows that. Yours isn't made to sit on, but to receive blows.

PLÁCIDO: Sometimes I think that you're a bit servile, in a word, an ass kisser.

EPIFANIO: I'll stand up so that you can see that there isn't anything to all that. (EPIFANIO *stands up*.) And now, what do you say to me? . . .

PLÁCIDO: If you want me to tell you the truth, you've lost a great deal of your true personality.

EPIFANIO: Well, and now what?

PLÁCIDO: What about what? . . .

EPIFANIO: What can you do when you stand up?

PLÁCIDO: It's what I was asking myself.

EPIFANIO: What do the masters do when they stand up?

PLÁCIDO: What do the masters do when they rest on you?

EPIFANIO: In order to find out . . . let me climb up on top of you.

PLÁCIDO: That's right! . . . In order to find out . . . let me climb up on you!

EPIFANIO: How do the masters speak when they make love on top of you?

PLÁCIDO: How do the masters laugh when they piss on you?

EPIFANIO: How do the masters pray when they shit on you?

     [Song of the Standing Poor]
PLÁCIDO: How do the masters speak,
    how do the masters laugh,
    how do the masters climb onto their
    faithful servants?
    What do I know?
    I only ask myself:
    and now that we're standing,
    and now that we're standing . . .
    What?

EPIFANIO: How do the masters sweat,
    how do the masters smell,
    what do the masters do
    in order to be charming?
    What do I know?
    I only ask myself:
    and now that we're standing,
    and now that we're standing . . .
    What?
PLÁCIDO: How do the masters swallow,
    how do the masters lie,
    how do the masters dance
    without their backs hurting them?
    What do I know!
    I only ask myself:
    and now that we're standing,
    and now that we're standing . . .
    What?

EPIFANIO: Well, friend, it isn't so bad! Now that we're standing, we can go to France. There, instead of being underdeveloped we shall be subdevelopé.

PLÁCIDO: I'd prefer to go to the capital. There instead of a young master, a whole corporation mounts you. Every little bit counts.

EPIFANIO: I don't know whether to surrender to alcohol, sex, or optimism.

PLÁCIDO: The only thing which consoles a little is being part of the country's folklore.

EPIFANIO: Things can change.

PLÁCIDO: The only changes that there have been in these lands were the earthquakes of the eighteenth century.

EPIFANIO: I trust in the future.

PLÁCIDO: My son says that he wants to be a delinquent, but I've told him that we don't have the means for that.

EPIFANIO: Delusions of grandeur.

PLÁCIDO: We will be poor, but honored not one whit. In order to rob decently, you must have a university education.

(*Shots and cries are heard again.*)

EPIFANIO: And that? . . .

PLÁCIDO: They're shouting something.

EPIFANIO: Disorders, tumults, it's already known.

PLÁCIDO: They're protesting. They're coming here.

EPIFANIO: If you put yourself in the middle, you'll lose.

PLÁCIDO: They want to change things.

EPIFANIO: In all these years we've gotten something, I say.

PLÁCIDO: It's true. And why lose it, just like that?

EPIFANIO: Do you know what I'm thinking?

PLÁCIDO: What? . . .

EPIFANIO: That more things are gotten when one is on all fours than when one is standing.

PLÁCIDO: And so? . . .

EPIFANIO: Perhaps it was a mistake to stand up.

PLÁCIDO: Perhaps. . . . (*The cries sound closer.*) What are they shouting?

EPIFANIO: Exploited of the world, unite!

PLÁCIDO: And what can that mean?

EPIFANIO: It sounds subversive.

PLÁCIDO: And who are they?

EPIFANIO: Adventurers, rabble . . .

PLÁCIDO: The only certain thing is that after someone defends us, he ends by getting on top of us.

EPIFANIO: Of course, it's easier to shout when you're on top of someone.

PLÁCIDO: If you'd pay me, I'd shout for you. . . .

EPIFANIO: And what would you shout if I'd pay you?

PLÁCIDO: Things like: Long live Epifanio! Justice for Epifanio!

EPIFANIO: I like it. Where will I be able to get the money to pay you?

(*The* GENTLEMAN *and the* LADY *enter.*)

GENTLEMAN (*to the* LADY): I took hold of that policeman by the lapels and told him face to face, "I've nothing more to add to my silence of the last twenty years," and he remained lost in thought.

LADY: What I say is: And the people who think . . . what do they think about? . . .

GENTLEMAN: Don't be morbid, Nene. . . . Why not be happy like the rest of the imbeciles?

(EPIFANIO *moves toward the masters.*)

EPIFANIO: Alms, for the love of God!

GENTLEMAN: How dare you mix God in a dirty matter of money?

(*The* LADY *gives* EPIFANIO *a coin.*)

LADY: Good man, it would please me beyond measure if you spent part of this money in seeing some good film by Antonioni.

EPIFANIO: Don't worry, miss. (EPIFANIO *moves forward again, insisting before the* GENTLEMAN.) Alms, for the love of Antonioni!

GENTLEMAN: Of course, fellow. . . . Do you have change for a hundred-dollar bill?

EPIFANIO: No, sir.

GENTLEMAN (*to the* LADY): If he had I'd have slapped him in the face.

(EPIFANIO *has approached* PLÁCIDO. *He shows him the coins.*)

EPIFANIO: Now I have money. Here, shout for me!

PLÁCIDO (*who takes the coins and shouts timidly*): Long live Epifanio! . . . Justice for Epifanio!

EPIFANIO: Louder! That's why I'm paying you!

PLÁCIDO (*shouting louder*): Justice for Epifanio! More bread for Epifanio!

EPIFANIO (*protesting*): I don't want bread!

PLÁCIDO (*shouting*): Less bread for Epifanio!

(*The* GENTLEMAN *and the* LADY *comment.*)

LADY: They're organizing themselves.

GENTLEMAN: It's amusing.

LADY: No, it isn't amusing. It's dangerous.

GENTLEMAN: When they stand up and begin to think, the best that can be done is to give them a poster so that they get it out of their systems.

LADY: And muzzle their brains! Let them shout all they want, but don't let them think. (*The* LADY *binds* PLÁCIDO's *head.*)

PLÁCIDO (*to* EPIFANIO): Now, all right. I'll not shout even one single demand of yours if you don't pay me again.

EPIFANIO: You know that I don't have any money.

PLÁCIDO: Beg!

EPIFANIO: Alms, for the love of social demands!

(*The* GENTLEMAN *gives a sign to each one.*)

GENTLEMAN: Here are your alms, good fellow.

(*One sign reads Long Live, and the other reads Down. The poor wretches read the signs and look at each other with hate.*)

PLÁCIDO: Pig! . . .

EPIFANIO: Cuckold! . . .

(*Each one leaves by a different side. The* GENTLEMAN *and the* LADY *sing.*)

	[Song of the Signs]
LADY:	If they stand up on two feet
	or if they want to rebel,
	if they comment in a low voice
	or if they begin to think . . .

LADY AND GENTLEMAN:	Give them a sign.
	Let them shout.
	Give them a sign.
	and let everything continue the same!

GENTLEMAN:	More caviar for our children!
	More champagne for our home!
	The yacht for he who has earned it!
	And to hell with the rest!

LADY AND GENTLEMAN:	Give them a sign.
	(*Same as above.*)

GENTLEMAN:	Justice for he who
	doubles his capital!
	We rich also want
	to have a chance!

LADY AND GENTLEMAN: Give them a sign.
                        (*Same as above.*)

(EPIFANIO *appears from stage right and* PLÁCIDO *from stage left. They meet face to face and remain motionless in an aggressive posture.* EPIFANIO *carries a completely blank sign.* PLÁCIDO *carries a sign on which is written in large letters Etcetera, Etcetera.*)

GENTLEMAN (*pointing at the sign*): How dare they suggest so much?

LADY: It's almost obscene! (*Calling.*) Censure!

GENTLEMAN: I've a friend in the censor's office, but he's very leftist.

LADY: They ought to forbid blank signs! They're disturbing.

GENTLEMAN (*shouting to them*): Subversives!

LADY (*shouting to them*): Antisocial! Corrupters!

GENTLEMAN (*shouting to them*): Anarchists!

LADY: At times I wonder if instead of poor they aren't just snobs.

GENTLEMAN: They're a couple of monopolists, speculators of poverty. They want it only for themselves.

LADY: They take everything literally. They want to use liberty in order to be free.

GENTLEMAN: And that's not liberty; it's license.

LADY: It's a problem of semantics, I say, and it has nothing to do with human rights.

GENTLEMAN: Human rights, human rights. . . . And I ask, when are they going to proclaim our rights?

LADY: The inhuman is always postponed. Don Justo! It's shameful.

GENTLEMAN: You're telling me!

LADY (*pointing to the poor wretches*): Look how still they are.

GENTLEMAN: Don't underestimate them, Nene. It just may happen that the standard of living is raised and we'll no longer be different from others.

LADY: I like to experience strong sensations, but I believe that this social solidarity has lasted too long now. I ought to begin to think of my health.

GENTLEMAN: It's true. Let's think of us!

LADY: I'd say: Let's think of them!

(*The* GENTLEMAN *gives* EPIFANIO *a sign on which is written Yes, and the* LADY *gives* PLÁCIDO *a sign on which is written No. Both poor wretches look at each other defiantly from the two ends of the stage and they advance toward one another in a very slow fashion. A moment of violent expectation while the two advance tensely and slowly. While this very slow movement takes place, the* GENTLEMAN *and the* LADY *sing, recite. In the meantime we hear music and records, explosions, and bursts of machine guns. The song recitation of the* LADY *and* GENTLEMAN *is whispered and rhythmic.*)

GENTLEMAN: They're so violent.

LADY: They're so uncivilized.

GENTLEMAN: They're so stupid.

LADY: They're so barbarous.

GENTLEMAN: They're so primitive.

LADY: They're so fanatic.

GENTLEMAN: They can't dialogue.

LADY: It's a pity.

GENTLEMAN: They can't coexist.

LADY: It's a pity.

GENTLEMAN: They can't collaborate.

LADY: It's a pity.

GENTLEMAN: They can't have freedom.

LADY: It's a pity.

GENTLEMAN: They can't have access to power. It'd be chaos.

LADY: It's a pity.

GENTLEMAN: They can't have access to culture. They're apathetic.

LADY: It's a pity:

GENTLEMAN: Yes, it's a pity.

(EPIFANIO *and* PLÁCIDO *have come very close to one another. They stop. They remain motionless for a few seconds looking at each other angrily. They then pound each other's heads with the signs.* EPIFANIO *falls.* PLÁCIDO *keeps on beating him.*)

GENTLEMAN: They're so uncivilized.

LADY: They're so . . . what would you say . . . so . . . so . . .

GENTLEMAN: They're like that.

EPIFANIO *(before dying)*: I am dying; therefore I exist! (*He dies.*)

GENTLEMAN: It's regrettable.

LADY: It is a . . . what would you say . . . a . . .

GENTLEMAN: Pity.

(PLÁCIDO *has remained with the destroyed sign in his hands, as though stunned.*)

GENTLEMAN: It seems as if Epifanio has died.

LADY: If he isn't dead he'd deserve to be for frightening me so.

GENTLEMAN: He always was *declassé!*

LADY: He always was intellectual.

GENTLEMAN: He always was a traitor to the proletariat.

LADY: A revisionist.

GENTLEMAN: One who sold out to imperialism.

LADY: Fortunately Plácido still has a strong back.

GENTLEMAN (*giving a sharp order*): Plácido!

(*In a completely automatic fashion,* PLÁCIDO *gets down on all fours. But then, in that position, he touches* EPIFANIO'*s body with his hands. He stands up again. The* GENTLEMAN *orders him again and snaps his fingers.*)

GENTLEMAN (*authoritatively*): Plácido!!

(*A new automatic movement of* PLÁCIDO *who gets down on all fours and then, as though driven by a slow force and almost in spite of himself, he begins to stand up very slowly as if he were a figure in a slow-motion film. The* GENTLEMAN'*s order is repeated. Again the poor wretch gets down on all fours, but this time in a much slower fashion than before. With the same slowness he stands up again.*)

GENTLEMAN (*authoritatively*): Plácido!!

(*Now the four actors break character and advance toward the audience and sing alternately to the audience. Perhaps only the* GENTLEMAN *should sing this, or the actor who does it best.*)

ACTORS (*singing*):
        How to finish this play,
        friends,
        this farce, how to finish it? . . .
        With Plácido on the floor
        and the Gentleman
        and the Lady mounted on his neck?
        Or with Plácido rebellious

standing
on his worn shoes?
We can end it
by machine-gunning everyone:
the Gentleman and the Lady
Plácido and the other one.
What to do with Plácido,
friends,
with the rich and the poor?
Will he resist the snapping of the fingers?
What do you think?
Will he do violence to his own story?
Here are the characters,
decide it!
Here is the voice of authority
and our daily temptation
to get down on all fours
and lick the executioner's ass.

(*The actors leave.*)

CURTAIN